Ingo Weigel

Self-Defense

For Modern Times

Ultimate Close Quarter Combat

Published by

Revat, Inc.

ISBN: 978-1-4116-6847-8

Table of Contents

Introduction

We are now living in the information age. The more information one can acquire the better he can adapt to ever-changing situations and circumstances. However, a normal day still only has 24 hours. In a time where information is the key to success, we need to find new ways of accelerated learning methods. Better and faster learning methods require better and more sophisticated learning programs.

This book will introduce you to Revat, a highly effective self-defense program that focuses on reflexive striking techniques. Revat training can compliment traditional martial arts, especially at the advanced levels. It fills the gap between the pre-contact stage of a fight and the fight on the ground. However, martial art training is not necessary or required in order to learn and apply Revat effectively.

Revat can be learned easily and offers great benefits for men and women living in an urban environment. Practitioners of Revat follow a unique and intelligent training curriculum in order to learn realistic and reliable self-defense that is effective and applicable for today's busy adults. On a more advanced level, we are going to take you on a journey that will strengthen your confidence and help you find inner peace, balance and power.

"Revat is a new and revolutionary self-defense and Personal Leadership program for urban professionals!"

Revat is not magic. It is the result of accelerated learning methods and a unique training program in combination with your efforts towards a higher understanding of the physical movements and techniques applicable in self-defense.

Living in the 21st century, it has become eminent for many people to become familiar with effective self-defense. Self-defense training enables you to stand up for what you believe in. It allows you to live your life without the fear of an attack, physically and verbally. You can use your self-defense training to make your own neighborhood a safer place to live in and raise a family. Imagine, if everyone in your neighborhood or town would have training in self-defense; wouldn't that make the town a much safer place?

In this book, you will discover the missing link to real personal safety. I believe in good education and in today's world, it includes education, knowledge and skills when it comes to personal safety.

We will bust many myths about martial arts, self-defense and how to deal with verbal and physical attacks on the street. You might be surprised about the things you can do to be safe. Once you have some training you will realize quickly how much you were hurting yourself before.

You may have noticed that today's attacks and crimes are much more violent and vicious than ever before. This is not so much a result from TV and video games we watch and play every day. The real reason is that we as a society allow this to happen and grow. We need to learn to stand up for our own safety and cannot rely on other people for that. We as people need to create a safe environment for our children to grow up. Therefore, we as people need to take action now!

The Reality of Self-Defense

"In real life, your attacker is always stronger!"

When I was younger, I had some friends who trained traditional martial arts; and they were good. They had won most of their competitive fights and they were well known for their skills in the ring. Then there was another group of people; people without any formal martial arts training. Nevertheless, do not think they did not know how to fight. Oh boy, they were good... and feared. There was absolutely no sense of fairness and rules. The only goal was to win. The people who had training in martial arts were used to rules and practiced accordingly. Naturally, they got into fights and were surprised when they lost against someone with no martial arts training. After all, they had formal training in fighting. How could they loose against someone without any training? The answer is simple: The reality of a self-defense situation is often very different from a competitive fight. Anything can happen, at any given time. Anybody who has ever been attacked knows that. There are only two rules that apply to every self-defense situation:

Rule #1:

"The attacker is always stronger than you are!"

Jennifer C.:

"Especially for a woman training in self-defense it's easy to realize this is true. This probably makes it easier for me to give way and deflect an attack. I do not expect to

use brute force to overpower my opponent. What I do get from this training (besides confidence) is core body strength, balance and coordination. I can deflect an attack, stick to it and return with a counter-attack in one motion."

It does not matter how strong or fit you are. You can be certain that your attacker is stronger; ALWAYS! Don't believe it? Let us assume for one moment that you are the attacker. If you were to attack someone random on the street, who would you pick? Would you pick the 300 lb person who looks like he is going to push you through the wall or would you pick the little guy who seems nervous and scared? I think the answer is obvious. Now, why would any other attacker do this differently?

If you are attacked then it probably is because the attacker sees an opportunity and thinks you are an easy target. If he is right or wrong does not make a difference anymore because he made up his mind. You are going to drive yourself crazy if you want to figure out why he attacked you. It does not matter and you need to let it go. It is happening and you have to deal with it, like it or not. A different attacker may have picked someone else – so what?

Some people want you to believe that it was you who provoked the attacker. Something you did (or did not do) made the attacker decide to attack you. Have you ever heard the phrase: "You need to be aware of your surroundings?" While this is a valid statement, it is not always applicable in a real life situation. Many times we are busy or preoccupied with other things such as an important meeting with a new client, a conversation with coworkers or friends or making sure our child doesn't run off at the mall. It is not always possible to be aware of a possible attack. Attacks normally happen when we least expect it; not when we are ready to defend ourselves. But here is the real problem: What if you are of your surroundings and you are aware of the thug approaching you to rob you or even hurt you. You can see him coming closer and you have this certain feeling that this is not going to be pretty. The real question you should ask yourself is: What do you do now? Running away is not an option for several reasons. Maybe it is too late to run away, or you do not want to leave your child behind or the bags are too heavy. Whatever the reason is, you know you need to do something to ensure your safety. Often times, screaming is not an option because there is nobody around to help you. What are you going to do now? This is why you need to have adequate training in real life self-defense. Self-defense training will enable you to control the situation and respond appropriately and calmly. A response may be verbally or physically, but you can be sure that you will be able to make the best decision and come out safe.

With Revat, you can learn how to deal with different attacks in various situations. The training prepares you for all kinds of real life self-defense situations. It offers the most complete self-defense curriculum. Going this route will assure you that you are always one step ahead of your attacker. That means, whichever attack he chooses you are prepared in advance and know exactly how to deal with it. It will feel like another training session for you because you have been practicing different possible scenarios in the classes.

As soon as the attacker realizes that you can protect yourself effectively and you are prepared to do so without being afraid he will reconsider and leave you alone.

Important: It is impossible to fake skills. I truly recommend getting some real training and not trying to pretend you know more than you actually do. You put at risk your own health. If you cannot back up your words and attitude, you are in deep trouble and you will pay for it. Be smart and make sure you only bit off what you actually can chew. Get real training and education.

Growing up I had a friend who loved martial arts. He was one of the best and had no problem defending himself. And he proved that several times. He always beat me in the friendly sparring fights we had. That was until I started taking my martial arts training in a different direction. I discovered quickly that it is possible to defend a stronger attacker and actually use his strength to my advantage. This experience has changed how I look at self-defense. It changed my life. I could tell that it was frustrating for my friend to experience the situation from the other side of the fence. I on the other hand enjoyed it very much. He started increasing his weight training and got even bigger. The funny part is the more he increased his training the easier it was for me to toy with him. Today, I enjoy working with people who have extensive martial arts training. They can see the benefits of Revat much sooner and it is easier for them to implement the different principles and techniques in their own training.

Rule #2:

The "2-Second-Rule"®

Jennifer C.:

"This is why training your mind and body to react instinctively is so important. Your response to an attack should be automatic. Reflexive! For a woman, these two seconds could save your life."

When you touch a hot stove, you do not need to think about what you should do next, right. You will let go immediately. When it comes to protecting yourself, you need to use the same reflexes. We all have those reflexes to protect ourselves. We just forgot about them because we started neglecting them. "if you don't use it, you'll loose it." This does not mean that you have to learn how to beat up other people. Far from it... Real self-defense gives you the ability to respond to a violent attack appropriately in a way you feel comfortable. Self-defense training teaches us to confront a problem, solve it and move on instead of ignoring it, and watch it escalate.

Do you remember the feeling when you are caught by surprise? It usually takes you a couple of seconds to realize what is happening. It is the same in a self-defense situation. You do not see the attacker sneaking up on you. At the very same moment you realize you are being attacked, you are already in the middle of the situation. That is exactly the moment when you already need to react and defend yourself without freaking out. You need to stay in control of your emotions and the situation.

The "2-Second-Rule"® states that you only have 2 seconds to react and defend yourself when attacked. Call it a sucker punch from behind, you did not see the thug attack you, the sun was in your eyes, they had weapons or whatever excuse you can think of. It may not even be an excuse and you are right with what you say. The bottom line is that you were attacked and hurt and the attacker got away with it while you are on your way to the Emergency Room. Even people with an extensive background in martial arts freeze when they get attacked in a real life situation. The Revat Reflex Training® is a unique and very effective trainings method to overcome the "freezing experience" and react instinctively without hesitation. Through this method, practitioners are able to react immediately and appropriately when they are attacked. The Revat Reflex Training® is the deciding piece in a fight and deserves its own chapter in this book.

"You only have a couple of seconds to defend yourself!"

I remember when I was living in Berlin. I was out with friends in a safe neighborhood. I left the bar around

3:00am and I was a little buzzed. A stranger approached me and asked me for money. I was reaching in my pockets when, out of the corner of my eyes I saw the guy taking a swing at me. The next thing I remember was the guy dropping on to the street from my punch. I was able to quickly react to the attack, defend it and counter it with a well-placed punch. All of this happened in a split second and the fight was over before it actually started. I did not have to think about what I would do if the guy would attack me and I didn't have to think twice about my defense when he actually did swing at me. At that moment, I was very happy that I was able to react and protect myself before I got hurt.

"You may train for a long time, but if you merely move your hands and feet and jump up and down like a puppet, learning karate is not very different from learning a dance. You will never reach the heart of the matter; you will fail to grasp the quintessence of karate-do."

Gichin Funakoshi
Founder of Shotokan Karate

"A black belt is nothing more than a belt that goes around your waist. Being a black belt is a state of mind and attitude. "

Rick English

What is Revat?

"Can you imagine that there is a program or exercise method to protect yourself against different kinds of physical and verbal attacks or assaults from a stronger and intimidating attacker? How would you feel if you knew that you actually could protect yourself and your family successfully? How would it change your life if you knew that you could go outside at any time, when you want to without having to worry about your safety? Can you imagine that this is possible?"

Revat is purely a practical self-defense and fitness program unlike any other. It is great for today's busy professionals, parents and travelers. Revat focuses on your ability to react appropriately and reflexively when in a potentially dangerous situation. Just like with the hot stove, it is the same when it comes to self-defense. Revat is not violent, but rather an effective method to deal with violence and protect yourself and your family when necessary.

"Knowing Revat gives you the peace of mind and the confidence to stand up for yourself!"

Knowing Revat gives you the peace and confidence to stand up for yourself and live your life free of fear and worry of physical abuse and attacks.

The techniques and movements are highly effective and very powerful. Adults of any age can learn and benefit from practicing Revat. The movements and exercises keep the body agile and the joints flexible. You will be able to relax muscles and muscle groups that are constantly in use during a day's activities. This will help prevent muscle, back and other pains, which can become chronic pains over time if ignored. Regular practice in Revat is like practicing yoga, meditation, core and strength training combined; you get better at it with every class. The best thing is that the exercises will keep you safe should you find yourself in a potentially dangerous situation.

The successful execution of the movements and techniques taught in Revat does not rely on physical attributes such as muscle strength and body height. It leverages these attributes and gives the "smaller" and "physically weaker" person a real advantage to protect him or herself.

When in a self-defense situation, the "victim" is always weaker than the attacker is and many times smaller. Nobody would ever attack someone who is stronger nor would a Zebra ever attack a lion. In other words, no matter how strong you are; if you ever get attacked you can be sure that the attacker is stronger than you are.

Revat training offers a full body workout and is a great way to strengthen your core muscles. The hand-to-hand coordination exercises are a fun challenge for every beginner and necessary in order to perform two (sometimes even three) techniques at the same time.

"With Revat you can live your life without the fear of being attacked!"

Every technique, every step and every kick in Revat is applicable and useful in a self-defense situation. We have eliminated unnecessary movements in order to increase the efficiency of the applications.

Do you have experience in another martial art? Revat can compliment traditional martial arts training due to its unique and specific training of the reflex system and the subconscious mind. This innovative reflex training allows practitioners of Revat to react to an attack using the tactile reflexes triggered through contact by the opponent. Every physical attack applies physical contact initiated by the attacker. Revat gives you the skills to react to this contact in a split second and turning this contact into your advantage. This contact is made with your arms. As a "victim", you naturally put your hands forward to protect yourself. In that position you always make contact with your arms first. Through this contact, you will know how much power is in the attack and the direction of the force. Revat training gives you the skills you need so you can take advantage of the attackers force, power and intention and control the situation and the outcome.

Randy F., M.D.:

"The goal of Revat training is to instill reflexive and effective techniques for self-defense. Describing Revat from a physical and psychological aspect can help explain its usefulness during an altercation. First the reflexive portion of Revat will be described, then the efficacy aspect and finally the psychological component.

When confronted, a potential victim's sympathetic nervous system will be activated. This will cause the commonly described "fight or flight" reaction. Obviously, "flight" (i.e. running away) is not always an option. If it were, there would never be any victims. If a potential victim cannot "fight" (i.e. defend themselves) their potential to become a victim increases significantly. While not responding, the victim might also experience a "deer in headlights" effect or "analysis paralysis" as they try to figure out what to do. Unfortunately, all of this occurs in a matter of seconds. Revat trains the body to respond to attacks automatically and quickly. When a cup of water is about to fall off a table most people just automatically reach for it without thinking about it or contemplating the consequences of grabbing it or not. This is the same principle applied in Revat. Therefore, situations are dealt with immediately and reflexively.

Unfortunately many have taken a weekend self-defense course where some "moves" are taught. If the victim is not comfortable with these "moves", they will not be used effectively. Often students blatantly forget what they learned; it is truly the antithesis of Reflex Training.

In Revat, repetition will create a muscle and neurologic memory that is always ready for self-defense without having to think about it. Conventional self-defense courses will teach a technique that will theoretically thwart the attacker. Unfortunately if that technique does not work the victim is then in harms way. In Revat, students are trained to continually defend and respond against attacks; therefore, a failed first defense/offense is inconsequential, as more will follow.

In regards to efficacy, it is useful to compare Revat to other methods of self-defense. In Revat, visual and tactile stimuli are used to assess the attack while in most other self-defense systems only visual ones are used. By increasing the information sent to the body, response times will decrease. The Revat practitioner actually tries to make contact with the attacker. The attack is automatically analyzed because of reflex training and is easily evaded. While visual assessment is helpful, the response time can often be too slow. Also, in Revat multiple actions happen at once. They could consist of multiple attacks or simultaneously sensing the attacker's moves and attacking. Other self-defense systems typically utilize one attack or one block at a time often occurring sequentially. This becomes obviously inefficient when one learns that multitasking is possible in self-defense. Combining the principles of utilizing multiple senses and multitasking creates a "how did you do that?" effect which can easily overwhelm an assailant.

Since Revat was designed with the assumption that the attacker is bigger and stronger, it needed to devise a way to increase the ability of the practitioner to create force. Newton's second law of physics describes force as equaling the product of mass and acceleration $(F=MA)$. When attacking using Revat the practitioner steps with their full weight behind it. A 125-pound person can *literally transfer most of that weight to the attack. Other self-defense systems rely on some transfer of weight into the attack but without actually moving the body, it is very difficult to utilize mass most efficiently. In Revat, the attacks are delivered with very relaxed muscles enabling more acceleration. If muscles are tense at all, opposing muscles work against each other to slow down the attack. Some people naturally have this tension in their punches but it can be eliminated. By utilizing one's entire weight behind the attack and by using maximum relaxation to create a whip like acceleration while attacking, the Revat practitioner is able to maximize the force generated. Revat takes advantage of the highly mobile nature of the shoulder and wrist joints for evasive maneuvering while taking advantage of stronger lower body and core muscles for stability. Many other self-defense systems do not rely on upper body flexibility but instead rely on strength while at the same time rely on the lower body for flexibility and speed. This would in effect be using the body for something that it was not designed to do."*

As a child, I was very impatient. I do not know how my parents were able to handle it. I always wanted to succeed right away. If something did not workout as I expected it, I would keep practicing until I got it right. I was very competitive, always wanted to win. I was looking for different ways to become better in my training. When I asked my teacher about it, he gave me the following answer: **"Don't focus on the things you don't have. Learn to be grateful for what you have and you will find what you are looking for!"** I had to think about it for a long time and I can see now what he meant.

"He, who has no patience, has nothing!"

Anonymous

Through Revat, I learned to control my emotions better which in return helps me to stay in control in stress situations. This ability translates naturally into the workplace. You will feel more confident when talking to clients, giving presentations and negotiating major deals. These are some of the benefits of Revat. Now let us talk more about the self-defense aspect and how Revat is different.

"Personal Safety can only come from within you!"

Revat is a fitness program that focuses on ultimate self-defense and personal safety. Your personal safety is your responsibility. Nobody else can be held responsible for your safety. It is an illusion to think or assume that someone else has to take care of your safety. If you put this responsibility in someone else's hands and something goes wrong then you pay for it with your health, even worse, you put other people like your family in danger.

For example:

You can surround your home with high walls and a top of the line alarm system, video surveillance... the whole nine yards. Now let us analyze this situation in more detail. You are living in a prison, a prison you created for yourself and your family. The price you pay is a piece of your freedom. Some people may say: "It is worth the price and I am happy to pay it!" Nevertheless, are you really safer? What happens when someone intrudes your prison? ... breaks into your house? What if someone attacks you outside of your home? ...on the way to or from work? ...while shopping? ...or while out with friends or family? What now?

As you can see, real personal safety and real confidence only comes from within you! Of course, you can and should add an alarm system to protect your home or your car but that is only to protect the property such as your home or your car! You need to make sure that you stay in control! Do not give the control/responsibility away to an alarm system, as it is only a tool. This tool can help you but it cannot do the work for you! You cannot foresee when and where you may be assaulted. Sure, you can be extremely cautious. However, as you also know, people usually are attacked when they least expect it. That means they are attacked when they feel very safe. How can you avoid this? You cannot! Let me repeat this: You cannot avoid it! It can happen at any time, anywhere. The best choice is learning how to deal with these situations. That brings us back to the reason why self-defense training is an important part of our lives.

If you know, if you are absolutely certain that you can protect yourself at any time, under any circumstances whatsoever, you develop a confidence that is rooted deep inside yourself which carries over in other aspects and areas of your life. It is with you all the time and nobody can ever take this away from you! You don't need to rely on anybody else or on anything else anymore. You create a safe environment for yourself and for your family.

"Less is More!"

Important: You cannot fake it! You cannot pretend to be someone else you are not. Any one of us is pretty good at sensing if someone is "real" or if someone is faking it; whatever it may be. **You only can fool another fool!**

You would not buy a car without test-driving it first. You would not believe the sales person that everything is fine and nothing will happen to the car. You want to test it. You want to check it out before committing to it. Because you know that if something goes wrong with the car, you will have to pay for the repair. My question now is: Why do you make a different choice when it comes to your personal safety? Why wouldn't you take simple and necessary precautious steps to protect yourself and your family? Why must something happen first before you make a smarter choice?

Of course, you can tell yourself nothing is going to happen to you! You will be fine! Don't worry. However, in the back of your mind you will always worry... You must change your negative thoughts of worry and fear and replace them with positive thoughts of confidence and skills. These new thoughts only come from the positive experiences that you gain from self-defense training.

Jennifer C.:

"Revat is reflexive self-defense. It trains the mind and body to react to threats in a fluid way that deflects attacks and uses an opponent's strength against them. Revat uses core body strength rather than muscle strength and sensitivity to contact in order to react to an opponent faster and with more force."

The Psychology of Self-Defense

If you believe we have evolved to modern and morally higher human beings, think again. There are numerous examples, which show that an effective self-defense program like REVAT is more important and appropriate today than ever before.

We all have heard about the recent attacks on American and British citizens in India. We certainly remember the attacks on 9/11 and the attacks in Spain. All of these have happened in the past seven years. These major international events show clearly that it can affect locals as well as business travelers. Professionals, who travel domestically and internationally for business and pleasure can certainly find themselves being involved in some kind of potentially dangerous situation.

Some people might be thinking: "Well, I rarely travel. How does this apply to me?" Well, just turn on the local News and you'll hear about the countless robberies, killings, rapes and batteries that occur in our neighborhoods almost daily; and these are neighborhoods in civilized industrial nations.

"Effective Self-Defense is more important today than ever before!"

Randy F., M.D.:

"When discussing the psychology of a physical altercation both the psychological factors of the attacker and potential victim need to be described. Humans are often guided by the psychological phenomena of "loss aversion". It has been shown that people fear losing

much more than they enjoy winning. Assuming there is not a "winner" in an attack we are just left with a potential loss. With that being the case whether to defend oneself or not becomes the issue. To do nothing is a guaranteed loss. To defend oneself is potential for loss aversion. Obviously, escaping an attack (i.e. running away) would be ideal but as stated earlier this is not always an option. Although an attack is never the fault of the victim, one should learn self-defense since, as Louis Pasteur stated, **"Chance favors the prepared mind"**. By learning Revat, one does not have to think about how to defend themselves or loved ones. It can, through proper training, be a natural response thereby eliminating psychological inhibitions.

To train in self-defense one has to emulate reality as much as possible. Many students that have not taken self-defense have a fear of hitting another person, as they are afraid to hurt them. These students will often hit very softly or not at all. In many self-defense programs, students use padding or learn to hit near their target but do not make contact. In realistic self-defense, one has to be comfortable hitting a non-padded target with no protective gloves. In Revat, students can train with and without gloves and make actual contact with fellow students. Less vulnerable areas of the body (e.g. upper chest) are chosen as targets in order to avoid injury but these targets are near very vulnerable areas (e.g. face and neck). Although not injured during practice students learn to not "freak out" when they actually hit or are hit by another person.

The psychology of the attacker should be considered when discussing self-defense. If an attacker is randomly seeking a victim, they will seek the path of least resistance. They will choose someone who is alone, unsuspecting and appears unable to defend themselves. While it is certainly encouraged to eliminate all possibilities of being attacked (e.g. travel in a group, always be aware of surroundings, etc.), it is not always plausible. Learning self-defense would be one of the last chances to discourage the attacker's travel down a path *of least resistance. Even if the attacker still chooses to attempt to victimize you, Revat has advantages over other self-defense systems. The Revat practitioner does not offer any resistance to the attacker (who is assumed to be stronger) therefore the altercation does not become a struggle of power. In Revat, one actually moves around a forceful attack. This can be disconcerting for the attacker because they feel as if they have completely missed their target (which they actually have). In addition, as mentioned earlier, Revat utilizes the principle of multitasking (multiple attacks at once). Combining the concepts of offering no resistance and multitasking will perplex the attacker in a situation where they are probably as scared as the victim."*

Jennifer C.:

"Revat self-defense isn't about being tough or aggressive. It is about building confidence and learning how to react in dangerous situations. Women should understand it is about taking control of themselves and their situation. It is about health, fitness, and confidence. It builds energy and endurance; it develops your core strength, balance and coordination. Its realistic self-defense training but you do not have to be big and strong or mean and aggressive. You will find that those things are easily used against your opponent. It is about being agile, quick, relaxed, fluid, and responsive - Reflexive! I often think it is like a dance. It is the development of your sensitivity, which allows you to react instinctively to your partner's or opponent's movements. OK, I may end up with a few bruises now and then, but it beats a treadmill any day."

"Revat is about building confidence!"

Being able to protect yourself is about learning new skills. Learning something new means we step outside our comfort zone and broaden our horizon, hence

'Personal Growth'. We have to work on our personal growth daily. If we stop, we die; maybe not physically, but mentally. It is like watching the same movie over and over and over again. At some point, we become sick of watching the same movie over and over and over again... and we let everyone know how sick we feel... we complain about everything and make everyone else responsible for our misery.

"Show me the people around you and
I'll tell you who you are."

If we want to know how the movie (our life) continues, we have to keep growing our minds. At some point during our training, we realize that we live in a wonderful world and we do not have to be afraid of anything. Finally, we get to enjoy the beauty of approaching strangers and sharing something wonderful with them. We see the world for what it truly is – a wonderful and loving place. Nothing can destroy this newly won image. If someone tries, well then you use your skills in a mature, responsible and appropriate way to let the other person know that they cannot harm you.

The Principles of Revat

Like any program of quality and value, Revat is based on principles and not rules. Rules usually do not leave much room for interpretation. They are solid. Principles on the other hand are much more flexible. When it comes to self-defense, positive results are very important. Principles are easier to adapt to a specific outcome.

"Revat is a Thinking-(Wo)Man's Program."

Practitioners of Revat are encouraged to think about the principles and their applications and how the techniques can be applied in specific situations. This helps you to understand what you are doing and why you are doing it. This newfound understanding is the foundation of effortless and explosive self-defense. It will be quite simple for you to apply the highly effective techniques without second-guessing your decisions.

"Revat is the Art of Solving Problems!"

The Revat program is based on six principles. These six principles are guidelines and references to the practical applications of the movements and techniques. Whenever you are in doubt about the practicality of a technique, you can check with these principles and find the answer.

Some of these principles may sound familiar. Their applications can be found in areas of our lives where strategic planning and competitive thinking are required.

The Military applies these principles as much as leaders and advisers in the corporate world. After all, the correct applications of these principles can be the deciding factor in all sorts of competitions. It does not matter, if we find ourselves in a battle over market shares, sports competitions or competing against ourselves. These principles always find their applications and can help us make better decisions.

"In Revat, practitioners think during their training so they don't have to think during a fight.

In conventional martial arts and self-defense programs, practitioners think during a fight, but not during their training."

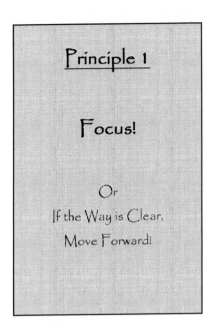

Principle 1

Focus!

Or
If the Way is Clear,
Move Forward!

The first principle is self-explanatory. It applies when you find yourself in a threatening situation and you have no other choice than to physically protect yourself. You can be sure that your attacker is stronger than you are. That means, just pushing him away is not going to be enough. You already told him to leave you alone and he ignored it. Therefore, you really have no other choice than taking control of the situation in order to protect yourself.

"If all else fails an offense is the best defense!"

This now is the time where the confrontation turns physical; you can feel it. You need to take matters in your own hands and protect yourself. You are ready to move forward and attack the thug if he only moves his little finger. If you miss this moment, you will find yourself being hurt one second later. With your attack, you will surprise the attacker. He does not expect you to take charge. The attacker expects you to be a "victim", cry, maybe scream for help, be afraid and go into fetal position. However, you do not give him this satisfaction. He will not know what is happening when you take charge and that is your best chance to control the situation and get out of it safely.

"Fight your enemy on their soil, not your own!"

The military has been using this very same strategy. It is better to fight a battle on enemy's soil. Using the strategy of a surprise attack often decides the battle in favor of the one who is proactive, even if the opponent seems to be superior.

Upstart companies apply this principle as well. How else can they tackle much larger and well-established companies? They find a weakness in an existing product or product line. It starts with an idea on how to do it better and more efficiently. Then they work on that niche until they establish themselves and can claim that territory. They do not wait until the larger company (opponent) has had the time to focus on that niche and improve it. It would be too late and the opportunity is history. Maybe some of you have had this kind of experience personally. Maybe you had an idea for a great product but did not follow through with that. Months later, you saw your product idea being advertised and available for purchase. Wouldn't it have been great if you had followed through with your idea and your name would be on that product? Imagine how your life would have changed. Then you realize what great opportunity slipped through your fingers by being indecisive.

When you are in a self-defense situation, you are experiencing the same symptoms. The only difference is that you will be physically harmed if you do not do anything about it. Remember, it was not your choice that you are attacked. You were chosen by someone else to be a victim. Now you are in this dangerous situation and the outcome depends entirely on your decision what to do next. You need to take charge and gain control. Otherwise, you will be controlled and it is not going to be pretty.

"If you don't design your own life plan, chances are you'll fall into someone else's plan. And guess what they have planned for you? Not much."

Jim Rohn
American Entrepreneur,
Author and Motivational Speaker

It is all about taking control. We cannot control the kind of situations we get in. However, what we can control is how we handle these different situations and what kind of decisions we make. Every new situation presents a challenge to grow and learn. It depends on the decision we make.

Some people want you to believe that all you need to do is tell the attacker to leave you alone and he will go away without harming you. Unfortunately, this kind of advice comes from people who have very little, if any experience and training in how to handle potentially dangerous situations.

If that would be reality then there would not be any crimes and assaults. The victims simply tell the attacker not to attack them and everything is fine. Of course, as intelligent human beings we know that this is far from reality. I personally think that the statement or advice: "If you are attacked just walk away!" is an insult and a slap in the face to anyone who has ever been attacked.

In the real world assaults, attacks and crimes still happen. That means attackers do not really care about what you have to say. Therefore, your arguments have to be more convincing. Sometimes, you have no choice than to physically protect yourself, if you want to or not.

It does not mean that you like or enjoy defending yourself and hitting someone else. Please remember, you will find yourself in a self-defense situation not by your own choice. Someone else chose you and now you have to deal with that and protect yourself, your wife, your girl friend or even your children.

The ability to protect yourself does not change who you are as a human being. Just because you can protect yourself does not mean you will start beating up everyone who crosses your path. All it means is that you are able to defend yourself physically and protect your family if all else fails and you have no other choice.

It gives you the control you are looking for and allows you to live your life without the fear of an attack.

"Power is the faculty or capacity to act, the strength and potency to accomplish something. It is the vital energy to make choices and decisions. It also includes the capacity to overcome deeply embedded habits and to cultivate higher, more effective ones."

Stephen R. Covey

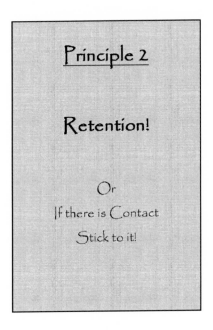

Principle 2

Retention!

Or
If there is Contact
Stick to it!

Here is where it gets interesting. In competitive fighting, both fighters test each other by throwing some jabs or light kicks. This is done to see how the opponent reacts to it. We refer to this as the "Pre-contact" stage of a fight. Not much is really happening. Each competitor tries to find an opening in the opponent's defense. Of course, this is true for competitions of any kind.

A real self-defense situation on the street usually does not offer the "Pre-contact" stage. The moment you realize that you are being attacked is when the attacker already is grabbing and holding on to you, maybe even pulling or pushing you. You have no time to think and consciously decide what your next move will be. If you have your reflexive movements trained you will be able react instinctively, appropriately and immediately without "freezing up". If you have to rely on your consciously made decisions, you will loose and get hurt. Let us be honest, that is exactly why an attacker approaches you out of nowhere. He does not want to give you any time to think. He also follows the principle of surprise.

Many self-defense programs and so-called experts completely neglect or ignore this. They want to teach you techniques or sell you products that will never work in a real situation. A technique is just that: a technique. It is your ability to react and apply that will make the difference in the outcome for you.

"Your safety does not depend so much on what you do. It depends much more on that you do something at the right moment!"

Applying Principle 2 means that you keep the contact that is initiated by the attacker. In order to keep this contact and react appropriately, you will need to have experience in the Revat Reflex Training.

Let us say the attacker punches you. Your hands are in front of your body or face to protect yourself. Now you get contact with the attacker's punching arm. Your arm immediately sticks to the attacker's arm like glue.

Through this contact, you will know exactly how much power is in the attack and the direction of the force behind it. This will allow you to use the attacker's force to move your body out of the way. Instead of blocking the punch you move the target (which is your face or body) so you do not get hit. Best of all, you use the attacker's force to move your body. A block is not going to work because the attacker is stronger and faster than you are. Should you be able to perform a blocking technique (which is highly unlikely because the punch is already coming at you) the punch will crush through your block because the force is greater than yours is.

This principle also applies if you were to punch the attacker and he blocks your punch. You also stick to his arm (block) and do not release the contact.

If the attacker tries to push you or grab you and you respond by pushing his arms away, you also have contact with the attacker's arms. You keep this contact for your own protection.

Through the specific Revat Reflex Training, you train your tactile reflexes to react to all kinds of different touches and attacks. The contact with the attacker's arms provides you with information about the power and strength, the direction and the target of the attack. You do not have to guess or anticipate what it might be; just "listen" to the information the attacker gives you. Through this way of receiving information, you learn to deal with what is actually happening. It eliminates otherwise possible fake attacks or theoretical attacks that never happen in a real situation. You are provided with information on what is happening at that moment. This information will trigger an appropriate response or defense that is successful, effective and most efficient.

In Military terms, it applies logically and naturally. Let us say you are ready for a battle and you can see the opposing army across the battlefield. You get the order to attack and start running across the field to fight the enemy. When the frontlines collide, the battle has begun and it ends when one army defeats the other army. You would not run across the field and as soon as you make contact with the opponent run back to where you started and see what happens. Besides the fact that this is hilarious, it is also extremely exhausting. No commanding officer or soldier in his or her right mind would ever think of this. When you make contact with the attacker stick to it!

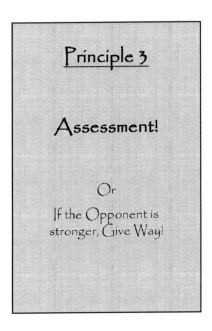

Principle 3

Assessment!

Or

If the Opponent is stronger, Give Way!

Now we have established that keeping the contact is a sophisticated and intelligent choice. Let us move on to the next principle. As mentioned earlier, through the physical contact of your arms with the attacker's arms you receive vital information you need to defend yourself in a split second. Before you made contact, you already had a feeling or even knew that the attacker is stronger than you are. The contact just confirmed it. Since you cannot move (block) the attacker's arm to the side (because he is stronger and his fist is already coming at you) you will use the energy of the attack to move your body out of the way. Just like when you jump out of the way when a car is coming at you. Keep in mind that you maintain the contact with the attack so you always know where the attacking arm is. The contact will transfer the energy of the attack from your opponent to you in order to move your body out of the way of the attack. It is like the attacker defeats his own attack by moving the target out of the way. All you have to do is let it happen and do not resist it. Your arms are always in front of your body like a shield protecting your body.

Actually, the shield is more modern like an Airbag. Imagine you have an airbag in front of your body. The attacker punches the airbag and deforms it. If you do not resist to the impact, your body will be moved and the airbag takes on its original shape. Another example is an air balloon. If you squeeze the balloon, it will give in at the point of contact and wrap itself around your finger.

What if the attacker uses a combination of attacks and follows his first punch with another punch immediately? Then you use your other arm and follow the same routine. You have two arms and so does your attacker. If you control both of his arms, he cannot harm you. If he does not attack you with his second arm then you can hit him (according to Principle 1). Of course, this requires actual training. At this point, we are establishing the theory and strategy of the movements in order to be more effective with the training.

This principle is quite logical. We apply it daily without doubting it. We walk around buildings and cars because we cannot move them. We all know that and nobody questions it. Why would it be different in a fight? Even in competitions, each fighter is trying to avoid being hit. They rely on their vision to signal an incoming attack. In a safe setting like a competition with one opponent right in front of you that may be all right. In real life situations, however this is not good enough. You do not know when someone will attack you; where someone will attack you and how many people will attack you. In reality, there is no safe setting unless you create this safety for yourself: PERSONAL SAFETY comes from within you.

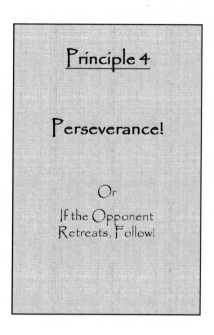

Principle 4

Perseverance!

Or

If the Opponent Retreats, Follow!

The fourth principle applies when the attacker is pulling his arm back after an attack (such as a punch). You made contact with his attacking arm and stuck with it. Now he pulls his arm back in order to launch another attack. You keep the contact and follow his arm going back towards him. Now your arm is very close to his body, face or whatever target you choose. Now you can release the contact and counter attack. You only have a split second to do this.

The Revat Reflex Training is a method to control the attacker and fend off his attacks. The goal is to attack your opponent without being hit in return. It is not an exchange of punches. You do not know how many punches you can take; therefore, you do not want to take any punches. It will be difficult for the attacker to hurt you because you are controlling his arms during the attack. In addition, before he launches another attack you seize the moment and counter attack. Now the attacker is defending your attacks and the situation has changed in your favor. You are in control now and can decide how to proceed. At that point, the attacker may decide to let go of you and run away. You have successfully protected yourself. Should he decide to continue then you also continue and the entire scenario repeats itself.

Important: The period for the situation described from the very beginning to the end is only a couple of seconds.

Street fights do not last several minutes. That is a misconception created by people who do not know what they are doing. Anyone who actually was attacked on the street knows that. The whole thing only lasts a couple of seconds. That is one of the reason, why many victims cannot remember details of what happened or what the thug looked like.

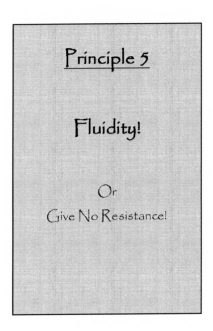

Principle 5

Fluidity!

Or

Give No Resistance!

Principles 5 and 6 are applied in the more advanced levels and become apparent in the Master Program of Revat. Principle 5 is actually a well-known principle. Whenever you argue with someone, you know that you have two choices.

Choice #1 is fueling the argument by persisting on your point of view and failing to recognize the point someone else is trying to make. You often can find it amongst children and adults who are being childish.

Choice #2 is recognizing someone else's point of view and trying to find a compromise that works for both parties.

How would that apply in a self-defense situation? Naturally, it has to find its application in exactly the same way as in a non-physical confrontation. After all, the situation is the same, a confrontation. One is verbal and the other is physical. Both are real situations and both can be solved by listening to the other person and finding a compromise. In a physical confrontation, "listening" to the attacker means finding out what he wants and then making a smart choice. If he is trying to hurt you then you want to make sure he understands this is not an option.

So, let us analyze the physical part of the confrontation. If the attacker punches and you only trying to block the punch then you are resisting to the force and the attack. You are telling the attacker to keep attacking you and you are telling yourself that you will continue trying to defend the attacks. You make the attacker stronger by putting him in control and you are making yourself weaker by putting yourself on the receiving end. A victim thinks like that and that is why they are a victim.

I do not care how many black belts you may have, eventually you will get hit. It is an illusion to think that you can defend yourself by trying to block all the attacks someone may throw at you. You cannot win a football game by keeping the ball on your side of the field. What makes you think that you can protect yourself by applying this hideous theory in a self-defense situation?

So, now let us say that you respond to the attack or punch with a block and a counter punch. This works nicely when you are in a safe class environment. However, in reality this will bring you in trouble. In a competition, your opponent is probably about as strong as you are, maybe even the same height and you both are in the same weight class. In addition, both of you follow the same rules and pretty much know the same techniques and movements.

The entire scenario changes in a street fight. There is no weight class distinction, the attacker is definitely stronger than you are and most likely, there is no bell to start the fight. You will know that you are attacked when you see the punch coming at you. Yet, you try to apply the rules from a controlled competition. What do you do if the attacker throws a combination of attacks at you?

Then you need to respond with a combination of blocks and we are back to you being the victim.

It is a much better choice if you do not give the attacker any resistance. You apply what you have learned so far. The attacker throws a punch at you. You make contact with the attacker's arm, feel the power and the direction of the attack, and use the power from the attack to move your body out of the way. You use that same power (or energy) for your counter attack against the attacker. Sounds simple, doesn't it? That is exactly, what you will gain from the Revat Reflex Training. This unique trainings method will train your tactile reflexes so you can do this too. It does not matter how much stronger the attacker is because you are not resisting to his force. You let his force pass and it cannot harm you.

"Your attacker is only as strong as you make him/allow him to be!"

Remember the example with the verbal argument. If you give in and are not stubborn about it, you can find a compromise and solve the problem. The same is true in a physical confrontation: If you are able to give in to the force coming at you and are not stubborn about it, you can find a compromise and end the fight without being harmed. Of course, this does not mean that you are supposed to take the abuse without doing anything about it.

Important: Energy cannot dissolve or disappear. It is always there. That means the energy or force coming at you from the attack has to be converted and redirected into something else. The smartest choice is to redirect the energy into the attacker's body instead of your own, don't you agree?

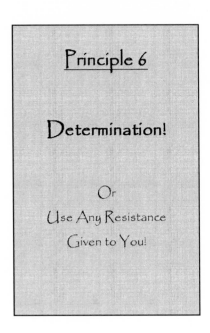

Principle 6

Determination!

Or
Use Any Resistance
Given to You!

Principle 6 is an extension of the previous principle. It may be difficult to accept in the beginning but once you have seen it in action and experienced it, it becomes obvious.

Applying this principle allows you to take advantage of any resistance you receive from your attacker. It is the highest principle and requires years of training and understanding. It gives you the ability to see your attacker's weaknesses and exploit them. You will be able to control the confrontation from the beginning to the end.

How long does it take to learn Revat?

If you want to be able to protect yourself when attacked, you should invest more than just a weekend. Revat Self-Defense is a skill that can be learned like any other skill.

Learning Revat is different. Although we offer group classes, instructions are still on an individual basis. The classes are small so every student receives the instructor's personal attention.

The Revat Technician Program (RTP) consists of ten levels. Each of these ten levels requires a certain number of classes. Your time commitment determines how long it will take you to complete the program. A certified instructor can help you achieve your goals in a time frame that works for you. On average, it takes about 12-18 months to complete the Technician Program. The good news is that you are able to protect yourself against all kinds of attacks in different situations successfully. If you are attacked in an elevator, at the airport, a public restroom, the Mall, a parking garage or even in your own home your safety will be increased with Revat. You will feel and be safer knowing that you can protect yourself and your family, if necessary no matter what the circumstances may be.

Most people start with Revat in order to learn self-defense. After a short time of training, they realize that their confidence also has increased. This is a direct result from our reality-based classes. We assume that you know already how to punch and kick. The challenge is in the overall coordination of simultaneous attacks and defenses. People with previous martial arts training find the different approach refreshing and challenging in a new way. It encourages letting go of old and outdated thinking patterns and replace them with a new, modern and more efficient structure. Beginners in Revat are encouraged to try anything they want or may have previously been taught. This helps the beginner to see what is effective and what is not.

In a typical Revat class, all kinds of realistic situations and applications are practiced. Of course, these drills depend on the student's level of progress. Gradually they advance to situations that are more complex.

Revat training in a safe and controlled environment improves the student's skills and increases their confidence. If a practitioner would ever be involved in a real life confrontation, it would feel like another training session.

This new and improved confidence can enable and help a Revat practitioner to take on new challenges in their professional and personal life. For instance, they may take on a new and difficult project, succeed and get the promotion; or they find their dream job, become an entrepreneur and start their own business. This new level of confidence may help them be comfortable approaching strangers at a party or on the street and asking out an attractive woman. They realize they can accomplish anything they want. All it takes is determination, skills, confidence and the desire to succeed.

REVAT and Traditional Martial Arts Training

Revat approaches self-defense and the close range fight from a different platform. Traditional martial arts and self-defense programs focus on the pre-contact stage and the fight on the ground. The pre-contact stage is when the two fighters are testing each other with jabs and kicks to see what the opponent does. This is very common in competitions. However, competitions have little to do with a real life self-defense situation. Competitions have rules, some more and some less. And even if it is agreed in advance that there are no rules in a competition there are always rules about not kicking or punching in specific areas of the body. Of course, this is to keep the competitors as safe as possible. Another rule is that the competitors know who their opponent is. They know exactly who they have to fight, where the opponent is and that no one else will interfere. They also know that they have to wait until they hear the bell and that the fight is over once they hear the bell again.

A self-defense situation is different from a competition. You usually do not know who is going to attack you, when someone is going to attack you and how many people are going to attack you. On top of all this comes the time of the attack... it often is the worst time possible. You might be out to dinner or on your way home. You may be preoccupied with a business proposal, a meeting or your kid's football practice. Suddenly, some thug is in front of you demanding your money. Before you can assess the situation, it is already over. There was no one who told you that this person is going to attack you. There was no bell

"The stronger the attacker is the easier it is to defend his attacks with Revat!"

signaling the beginning of the first round. In addition, you were not sure, if this person was alone or if there was a group of attackers. The entire scenario only lasted a couple of seconds...

Revat teaches you what to do after the contact is made and before the fight goes to the ground. It enables you to react in a split second and respond to an attacker with appropriate force. All of this happens without that you have to make a conscious decision about what to do. You react and respond instinctively, appropriately, reflexively and decisively. That is what Revat is about. It does not matter if the attacker is stronger or taller than you are, if he attacks you in a dark alley or in the middle of your lunch break. You will stay in control with Revat.

"The stronger the attacker is the easier it is to defend his attacks with Revat!"

Jennifer C.:

"Revat trains your body and mind to react instinctively to a threatening movement or attack. Other self-defense training offers tips on what you should do if you are attacked. They tell you to carry personal alarms, little flashlights, use your keys or even your purse as weapons. They tell you to scream or kick and to run, but at that moment when you are attacked do you feel confident that you will remember these things or make the right decision? Most likely, you will be caught off-guard; someone will come up on you from behind. You will be shocked, confused, and scared. Revat trains your reflexes. Your defenses are instinctual. You will be able to react before your attacker gets that close to you. You have two seconds, do you really have time to think about it or will you have already taken him down?"

Revat is not necessarily considered a traditional martial art. It is purely a self-defense program with a complete self-defense curriculum including various attacks in any of the five distances.

Traditional martial arts offer a great way to learn about the history of a specific art, its techniques, strategies and fighting priorities. It does take many years to master a martial art (minimum is 10 to 15 years of daily practice for several hours). In many arts, the first degree black belt is not even considered a Master Level, but rather the entry level to Mastery. Practitioners need to achieve a minimum of a 5th degree black belt in order to deserve the title of a Master.

The structure of the Revat program is very different. The purpose for Revat is to teach realistic self-defense in the shortest time possible. Do not be fooled, Revat still requires training and practice. You learn effective self-defense from the first day on forward. The entire curriculum focuses on effective self-defense training, situations and applications. With Revat, there is no need to study for several years before being able to defend yourself successfully. The requirements to learn Revat are higher than for other programs.

"Revat teaches you effective self-defense in the shortest time possible!"

Traditional martial arts teach you technique after technique. You may learn many of them and you probably will forget most of them unless you practice hard every day. Here is an open secret. Adding more and more techniques does not make you safer. Actually, it makes you more vulnerable. Techniques are like tools you purchase at a hardware store. You can purchase the entire store with thousands of tools. However, if you do not know how to handle them they are useless; shiny but useless. You need to learn how to use the tool and understand its purpose. It is the same with a technique.

Important: Techniques are stored in the conscious brain. You need to remember them. Reflexes are stored in the subconscious brain. You do not need to remember them. Therefore, you do not loose time through thinking and deciding which technique you should use in a dangerous situation. With a well-trained reflex, you will always *react* automatically, appropriately and instantly.

The unique and innovative Revat Reflex Training trains your reflexive responses to an attack, your subconscious mind and your nervous system. It is here where techniques are turned into reflexes. That makes Revat a great addition to traditional martial arts training. It can enhance the effectiveness of traditional and today's mixed martial arts and reduce the time of practice before you are an effective fighter.

"Conventional martial arts and self-defense programs put you in a victim position!"

Especially women can benefit from Revat training. Just like Renee, women get to experience first hand, how effective and powerful they become with Revat. When Renee came to Chicago, she started looking into taking self-defense classes. She had never heard of Revat before, but among the choices, she found on the internet, it seemed to speak to her. Not until she took some classes did she realize what really drew her to the program. "Revat, unlike other self-defense courses, does not initially put you in the role of a victim", she said.

From what Renee had experienced of other self-defense courses, participants are given situations where they were being victimized. They learned techniques that were supposed to get them out of those situations. Many times, these techniques did not work and the training left the participants confused and insecure. Participants did not think they had any control of the situation. It always started and stopped with the technique itself, and logic would then demand that the next step would be to run like hell. However, what happens when you cannot run? What happens when the attacker does not do that exact hold in the exact way as it was shown in class? Most likely participants would freeze and end up in just as bad a situation as if they knew nothing from that self-defense course. What Revat gives its practitioners is different. *"You come to these situations not as the victim, but from a place of control. The attacker may make the first move, but with Revat, you will reflexively know what to do. Your subconscious mind takes over. It is like playing catch. When you first started, you would miss, drop it or dodge it, but once you got the hang of it you would step in to grab it and then use its momentum to throw it back. Revat teaches you to do that with a punch: Deflection and reflection. You don't have to be the stronger one if you are sending their energy right back at them."*

Helen describes her experience with Revat: *"Living in Chicago can sometimes be daunting for a single woman. I realized that, and wanted to do something about it. By taking Revat classes, I realize that even if I never have to apply my training it gives me confidence in my ability to realistically protect myself; which then in turn, gives me the outward appearance of strength that deters others from seeing an easy target. Revat demands that you become aware of yourself and it shows you how you react in a stress situation. Part of the training is unlearning deeply ingrained habits, and rewiring your brain to act in a more productive way. These skills take you from a self victimizing attitude to one of self control and self reliance, and can be applied to all aspects of your life."*

Technique vs. Reflex

Which technique does the brain use to think? Which technique does the tree use to bend with the wind? Which technique does the water use to flow? None. However, it happens anyway. Maybe techniques are not the right answer.

It is important to understand the difference between a technique and a reflex as it explains why techniques are not the answer to effective self-defense. Some people seem to think the more techniques they know the safer they are. On the contrary - **Less is more!**

What is a technique?

A technique is like a tool. You need to learn how to use this tool. If you do not know how to use the tool properly, it is useless to you. In order to apply a technique you must make a conscious decision. That means you have an outside impulse (i.e.: a punch coming towards your face). Your eyes register this attack as danger and send a signal to your brain. Your brain now has to make a quick decision on what to do next. The brain may decide to block the punch with the right arm; or it decides to block with the left arm. Here is already a conflict that influences the execution of the defense. Now, the punch also could turn into a low punch or stop completely (fake punch) and the attacker now attacks you with the other arm or even a kick. For each attack are at least two options for

"Collecting techniques is like collecting belts – neither makes you a better fighter!"

a defense. Do you defend it with your left arm or leg or with your right arm or leg. Now you can see why many people are in a lot of trouble with their timing. Unless you have many years of daily training, it is almost impossible to pick the right defense at the right time. As for many people, by the time they see a sign of an attack, the attack is already coming at them with full speed. Their instincts tell them what to do. The problem for those people is either their instincts tell them nothing or the lack of confidence and trust in their instincts makes them "freeze up". They have not been trained to react. Their training consists of predetermined attacks and predetermined defenses. That is why certain moves work well in training but never in reality.

Traditional self-defense programs do not teach you to react to an attack. They teach you to act on an attack. This is a very important difference since it has a direct impact on the outcome (your safety). The defender acts on an attack and when the defender is wrong, he gets punched in the face.

This is not so much the defender's fault. The fault is with the technique and the training of it. You are forced to choose out of many techniques the one that works in a split second while the attack is already coming at you. Even well trained martial arts practitioners have problems with this.

What is a reflex?

A reflex determines how you move and react to an outside impulse without having to make a conscious decision. For example, when you touch a hot stove or the power outlet in the wall, you do not have to decide what you should do next. Should you hold on or let go? You immediately let go without a question. You do not have to think about it and you always do the right thing.

This kind of reaction is rooted in your subconscious mind. You have learned to react through trial and error.

You probably have touched something very hot at some point in your life and this memory is still with you. Can you imagine how simple self-defense can be if you have good reflexes to rely on when attacked? You would always react appropriately to an attack and it would always work. You would not have to second-guess your reaction because you know it is perfect.

That is exactly what you'll gain from Revat. Revat teaches you reflexive movements that will be stored in your subconscious mind. You do not have to worry if you will remember them when needed. Of course, you will; just as you remember to let go of the stove when it is hot.

You also know that you have these reflexes always with you, no matter if you are on an airplane or in an elevator, if you are shopping at the Mall or enjoy a dinner with friends. It even goes so far that your mind can focus on something else, talk about different things and you will still be able to defend attacks and control an attacker. You do not need to see an attack because you have learned to rely on your tactile reflexes.

Revat practitioners often talk about business, family, politics or whatever is on their mind during their training. Is the training still effective? You bet it is. It is the subconscious mind that is being trained not the conscious mind. The subconscious mind keeps you safe and enables you to react in a split second. The subconscious mind eliminates the moment of "freezing" when you are attacked by surprise.

Important: In a stress situation, you only can rely on your reflexes. You will have to react in a split second and you need good reflexes.

Self-Defense and Weapons

Knowing Revat eliminates the need to own a weapon for the purpose of self-defense when living in an urban environment. I personally do not recommend owning a weapon when living in a large city to protect yourself for several reasons. One reason is that a weapon escalates the situation to a completely different level. When a weapon is involved, you are fighting for your survival and nothing less. At that point, you cannot be worried about your new expensive suit or the $500 cash in your wallet. Your only concern is to survive. If you bring a knife into the confrontation then your attacker may have a bigger knife or even a gun. What are you going to do now? Why would you increase the risk by having a weapon? It is much smarter to go through the Revat training so you do not need to rely on additional weapons. Besides, you will not have the time to get your weapon out on time. Remember, you only have a couple of seconds.

Another aspect is the actual training. Yes, owning and handling a weapon also requires regular training. Either way, you have to get training. It is smarter to get training in weaponless self-defense first because it keeps you safe at any time and all the time. If you would choose a weapon you would have to make sure that this weapon is always with you

"A weapon will not protect you as much as your ability to protect yourself!"

and that you have easy access to it. In that case, what would you do at the airport, in an elevator or during your lunch break? Hope that nothing is going to happen?

Here is an interesting example: Let us assume you are on your way home after a night out. It is 2 or 3am in the morning and there is nobody on the street. You have some sort of a weapon with you to protect yourself in case of an attack, may it be mace or a pocketknife. You are most concerned because you have heard of a few attacks that have recently happened to other people in your neighborhood. You want to be prepared and therefore carry your weapon in your hand to save time. Now someone approaches you to ask you a harmless question. Maybe that person is lost and needs directions and you are standing there with your weapon ready. How would you feel if you were the one approaching someone else and seeing a weapon ready in that person's hand? What would you be thinking if they told you that the weapon is only for self-defense? Would you believe it? Would you start screaming, maybe even calling the police? What would you do?

As you can see, only the sight of a weapon in someone's hand escalated a situation to a completely new level and you actually feel threatened.

Jennifer C.:

"If someone attacks you, most likely they are going to have some form of weapon. It is important to train and have different people attack you with these weapons in order to know what it is like to have someone swing a stick at you or come at you with a knife. You are able to overcome that fear and learn how to react to the attack."

Close Quarter Concepts of Revat and Firearms

Many people, when they think of protecting their home and family, consider buying a firearm. The logic of such an acquisition is compelling; simplicity, easy of use, firepower and the finality of results. The role of guns in our history is profound and historically well documented. "The right to bear arms" is embedded in our constitution, and the very notion of freedom and liberty is closely associated with firearms. Guns are considered equalizers for all people. Anybody, regardless of status, size or physical power becomes a potentially formidable threat when in possession of a firearm. Given the availability and prominence of guns in our society, some of you may scoff at the need to train in weaponless self-defense / martial arts. Why spend years of time and commitment to forge our body's minds and spirits in the ways of the warrior when all one has to do is acquire a firearm?

"Many martial arts styles and self-defense programs are impractical for the average civilian!"

You need to realize that firearms are just tools, and that with such powerful tools comes great responsibility. Powerful tools such as firearms, used without proper training and in the wrong way can become a threat to both the user and society. Legal issues, safety issues, control and effective deployment and use of such tools is critical to the existence of a safe, secure and functional society.

If specialized training and instructions at various levels such as beginner, intermediate and advanced would not be important and necessary then why do our elite protection agencies of society such as law enforcement groups and military forces engage so extensively in it? The prestige and reputation of various agencies is distinguished by the amount and type of training each has received. Special military forces such as army rangers and navy seals are held in higher regard than the average soldier because of their higher level of training. For the same reason the FBI and the Secret Service is held in higher regard and status than the average municipal police officer.

As a private citizen, it is our responsibility and duty to engage in regular training to understand the responsibilities of owning and handling firearms.

If you live in an urban environment and find yourself in a situation where you need to defend yourself against an attacker, many times it is not the best choice to use a firearm. First, you need to make sure that you can legally carry a weapon. Please keep in mind that you can shoot someone across a distance and you can get shot from a distance. I am not sure that allowing every civilian to carry a firearm will make the city a safer place. That is a different discussion for another time.

The next step is that you usually do not have the time to pull out a firearm when you are attacked. There is no time – remember the "2-Second-Rule". However, all that is not the most important factor in this equation. The most important factor is your skill and ability to handle a firearm. Let us say you can legally carry a firearm and furthermore you somehow managed to pull the gun when you were attacked. You are pointing the gun at your attacker and you tell him "Freeze, Dirt bag!" ...and he does not follow your command. What do you do now? Are you going to pull the trigger? There are two aspects I'd like to mention at this point.

The first aspect is your skill to handle the firearm and shoot the target. Can you hit the target in this high stress situation under the enormous pressure you will be feeling? Have you had extensive training where you were put in a high-pressure situation and all you could do was follow your instinct and kill the target? There is nobody else around you who will tell you what to do. You are on your own and fully responsible for your actions (just like any law enforcement officer). You screw this up and you may go to jail because you shot an innocent person. Maybe the attacker did not have a weapon and you shot him anyway because you lost control over your emotions and the situation. Maybe the attacker had a weapon and you pulled the trigger. But your training is almost none existing so you missed the target and killed a bystander, maybe even a child. This is not self-defense anymore; you just killed someone! How are you going to explain this to the victim's family and parents, and your family and maybe even your children? Is this the role model you want your children to look up to? And to put things more in prospective – once you pull the trigger you can be certain that the attacker will start shooting as well. If he knows how to shoot he will kill you. If he is as bad a shooter as you are than both of you will probably be shooting at innocent people around you. Both of you will kill innocent people and both of you completely screwed up. Think about that for a moment.

The other aspect is the question whether you are actually able to shoot a human being. Have you ever shot someone? Have you ever shot an animal? Many of the people who own firearms are not able to shoot an animal. So, why even having a firearm for self-defense? Law enforcement agents undergo psychic evaluation and possibly treatment after being involved in a shooting. Therefore, what makes us civilians with a regular 9-5 job think that we are able to handle the same responsibilities as a specially trained law enforcement agent?

Of course, this is something to think about when you live in an urban environment. People who live in the country close to the hunting grounds of wild animals should consider having a firearm for their safety and protection from animal attacks. Being attacked by a bear or being attacked by some thug on the street are two very different situations. They need to be treated differently.

Comparing the Principles of Revat and Firearms

From a self-defense standpoint, a gun is a relatively simple yet sophisticated tool for firing a small projectile at a high velocity to penetrate a target (assailant) with a straight trajectory and cause significant "fight stopping" damage to the assailant. Indeed most practical firearms self defense schools teach firing more than one bullet, usually two aimed shots, to the cardio-thoracic region in what is usually referred to as a "controlled pair" or a "double tap".

In a similar fashion, Revat is an unarmed program designed to achieve similar results. Revat trains the body to operate like a firearm. The hands accelerate explosively along a straight path to the target with the centerline analogous to the barrel of a gun. The forward steps serve as the gunpowder, or charge for the projectiles, as well as being the flight path for the attacks. In addition to the hands being likened to bullets, they can also be viewed as soldiers fighting in battle. The front hand is used to one's perimeter defense. The value in guns and soldiers for self-defense is actually in their offensive firepower to protect targets. Similarly, in Revat, when the limbs (i.e. the hands) are sent into "battle" and hand attacks are "chained" together, an "army" is created.

"Revat trains the body to operate like a firearm!"

The invention of guns and firearms changed the whole philosophy and approach of warfare. In Medieval times, very heavy body armor was necessary to protect one's targets and consequently large heavy weapons such as the claymore broadswords and heavy battle maces were used to penetrate this heavy body armor. Mass and power were the order of the day. With combatants dressed in body armor, empty hand attacks were just not practical at that time. The advent of firearms rendered bulky metal armor obsolete as well as the use of heavy hand weapons for warfare. Rapiers, sabers, light clothing, hand held muskets and cavalry, evolved and developed. Speed and mobility became more important, and in that regard, fencing was the principle swordplay that came into being.

Ironically, because of those developments that were set into motion by firearms, modern empty hand boxing became a practical supplement and alternative means of self-defense. Straight combination hitting, falling steps and shorter upright mobile stances became the foundation for modern empty hand combat.

Revat is designed much like today's modern firearms. It stresses great mobility with its footwork and puts emphasis on rapid rate of firepower. Chain punching in Revat can be likened to a machine gun, and with its fast and flexible footwork, it simulates a mounted machine gun on a mobile turret. Additionally, much the low thrusting kicks can be likened to a pump action shotgun, with their powerful blast like effects on the mid section, thighs, knees, shins and insteps of an enemy.

Revat Training to Supplement Firearms

As previously mentioned, complete, total self-defense based entirely on firearms is not sufficient or even adequate for today's needs. It has been well documented that determined criminal assailants when taken by surprise in close quarters have disarmed many times a law enforcement officer. There has been much discussion on weapon retention techniques and programs. These in fact, constitute a study of martial arts. It is also known that many savvy law enforcement officers, carry a backup smaller pistol, in the event that their primary firearm fails, or is lost to them. In similar fashion, we in the civilian world can only learn and emulate from our better-trained brethren. While the average citizen may not go on daily or weekly military or paramilitary maneuvers, martial art training is an undervalued, misunderstood and unappreciated tool for survival.

"Personal Safety based on Firearms only is by far not sufficient!"

"The preservation and protection of our health" are foundations of our very existence here in this world. It is known that the law of nature is harsh, and the so-called civilized human world is no different at its core. Just like wild nature, human predators and prey abound. In every sphere of being, it is important to know where one is and to hone our instincts and intuition; to avoid, escape and, if necessary, fight predators. Self-protection and the protection of our family, loved ones and nation are primal instincts, desires, and responsibilities of everyone. Military and law enforcement are there to supplement our self-protection needs, not the reverse. Learning the ways of the warrior are necessary skills to our survival and growth, for we are all on the "food chain" whether we are aware of it or not.

In some states of our country, it is relatively easy to legally acquire a firearm for hunting or self-protection. In fact, more states allow a concealed handgun permit for law-abiding citizens. Even in these states, where people have exercised their rights to possess firearms, it is not always practical or convenient to carry a firearm. In addition, within a radius of 5-10 feet, even with good training, unless one's firearm is already deployed (in practical shooting terms "at the ready"), it is quite likely not a useable option against a fast approaching and aggressive assailant. In what is a surprise to many, if your handgun is holstered and a fast moving attacker armed with a knife charges in from a distance of less than 22 feet, it is nearly impossible, even for a highly trained practical shooter, to shoot the assailant and defeat the attack before the assailant and his knife have done their likely lethal damage. Additionally, in a close encounter, there is a real risk that an attacker can wrestle away a firearm and use it against its owner. In addition, not every self-defense situation legally and morally justifies the lethal, final results that firearms produce. Revat training gives the user many greater options of control.

"In close range distance, a knife attack is often times more dangerous than a firearm!"

Similar to veteran police officers and warriors, Revat training is the "backup pistol" we all need to invest in our survival and well-being. In this regard, Revat is the perfect addition to every modern, contemporary citizen. Besides the aforementioned technical features that virtually make Revat resemble a gun, the accompanying physical and spiritual training of the program makes it the best value of this century.

People of modest physical talent and ability can effectively and readily employ Revat to protect themselves and improve the quality of their lives on a daily basis. Not every martial arts style or self-defense program can truthfully make this claim. Many styles and systems require excessive physical power and ability, rendering them impractical for the average civilian. The Revat program is fun, logical and trains students on multi-levels in a short period. The training strengthens the body and the balance of body and mind, and hone ones physical, mental and spiritual abilities. Strategy and tactical skills are also taught, and these are further integrated into an understanding of philosophical and legal arenas.

"Firearms can be effective if you know how to access and retain them!"

Revat is based on an ingenious integration of mathematics, physics and philosophy. It continues to grow and evolve based on its scientific, spiritual and philosophical roots.

In summary, firearms are effective self-defense tools but you may need Revat training to access and retain your firearm. In addition, firearms are less applicable in larger cities, crowded places, airports and shopping malls. For that, you will prefer training in Revat. Do you have your firearm ready at this moment?

Is Self-Defense Violent?

Some people with little experience and knowledge about the subject think that self-defense is violent. The truth is it is not violent but rather a way to deal with violence. The real question you should ask yourself is: "What are you willing and able to do when you are forced to protect yourself and your family? What value do you put on your personal safety and on the safety of your family and children?"

See, if someone attacks you then you are referred to as 'the victim'. That means you did not initiate the attack. You were chosen by someone else to be attacked. At the moment of the attack, the thug is ready to inflict harm on you and you are in no position to withdraw and say "I don't want to harm you". It does not stop the attacker; actually, it probably encourages the attacker because he can sense your increasing fear. You are not going to do anything about it anyway, so why should he stop?

"Self-Defense is not about violence. It is about your ability to deal with violence!"

Effective self-defense training puts you in control of the situation! That means you control the outcome. You respond appropriately, mentally and physically if necessary. You did not start the fight but you will certainly end it. If someone forces you to defend yourself, you will do so in the most appropriate and most effective way! Remember: It was not your choice to be attacked. However, it is your choice to be the victim or not!

Let us look at the myth that you should protect yourself without a physical fight. Virtually everyone who has ever studied martial arts has done that for one reason and one reason only: They learn how to fight and protect themselves! After years of daily training and becoming a master in the physical part of the martial art, some of them continued their studies and training on the spiritual and philosophical level. Somewhere along that path, these masters realized that the physical fight is very basic. They prefer not to fight but rather continue with their training and studies. If threatened or even attacked they probably choose not to use their skills and rather walk away from the situation or confrontation. However, and that is very important: They have the skills, the training, the mindset and the ability to protect themselves physically if necessary.

You only can afford to walk away from a confrontation or even a physical attack if you have the training and the skills to protect yourself physically if needed. If you do not have these skills and the training then you do not have a choice and you will always be the victim – by your own choice.

Jennifer C.:

"Learning self-defense is not about violence. It is about building confidence and knowing how to protect yourself. Self-defense is empowerment. While your opponent is always going to be bigger and stronger than you are, you know how to react and how to use their strength against them. You know how to be quicker and apply enough force to overcome them. Self-defense is about coordination, balance and reflex."

Courage – or The Ability to Speak Your Mind

As already mentioned in the previous chapter, it is not always possible to walk away from a confrontation or even less from a fight. It actually is very careless and just wrong to suggest that you should walk away and do not get involved. As mature adults in our society, we should be able to stand up for something we believe. If you see injustice happening either to yourself or to someone else you need to stand up and offer help and support to the person who needs it. By turning away, walking away and choosing not to help we become part of the problem; we become a passive attacker and empower the thug. Some day it will happen to you and you wish that someone would help you when you need it.

"When you are in a self-defense situation you don't have the choice to walk away!

There is also a myth out there that you can always walk away from a fight or a confrontation. Walking away is the coward's way to deal with an unwanted situation. It is being ignorant and selfish. Choosing to stand up and help is the better choice. Help and support do not always end in a physical fight, but if there is no other way you won't feel helpless with Revat. You still can offer your help to someone in need.

If a victim would have been able to walk away then there would not be any crimes!"

Important: It is not possible to walk away when being attacked. Otherwise, there would be no crimes, assaults, rapes etc. because the victims could have walked away from the situation. In fact, it suggests that the victims chose not to walk away and therefore chose to be attacked. Of course, this is ridiculous and just plain wrong. Anyone who has been a victim in one way or another should learn Revat to empower him or herself so that it never happens again. Avoiding certain places or situations is not the solution because anyone can be the victim of an attack, at any time and in any place. It comes back to the questions: Who is in control of your life?

"The idea of walking away disables us to solve problems!"

Here is another thought. Practitioners of martial arts have made a decision to study martial arts based on their inability to protect and defend themselves. The desire to effectively protect themselves is the reason why people start with martial arts. After years of training, study and experience, they reach a level of mastery in their art. At that point, they have gained the strength, the wisdom and the ability to determine that a physical fight is not always necessary and the best solution. However, and that is important, if they ever have to use their skills to end a physical confrontation before it escalates they will do so in a heartbeat without hesitation.

What does that mean? Masters of martial arts can operate on both levels, the verbal and the physical level. They know exactly what will happen to the attacker or offender if the confrontation becomes physical. Therefore, they always opt for ending the confrontation verbally. However, make no mistake; they are in charge of the situation, not the attacker!

Another aspect are the values you portrait. If you teach your children to walk away from a confrontation, what exactly are you teaching them? I am talking about confrontations among children in the schoolyard or playground and not about the extreme and serious situations where children are helpless and need the help from adults.

If you tell a child to always walk away from a confrontation then that is how they grow up. Where does this lead to? It leads to the child's inability to deal with confrontations and make a decision on their own. Instead, they will always blame someone else for their misfortune and never take responsibility for their actions or decisions made. They will probably find the real world harsh and cruel and have a difficult time to succeed. Success comes through winning. Winning is a result of healthy competition. Confrontations are part of competitions. I am not talking about physical confrontations. Competition is very important in our lives. We compete every day. Our biggest opponent is in our mind, is the voice that tells us we cannot do something. If we listen to this voice we limit ourselves, we prevent ourselves from achieving our goals. We have to learn to overcome our fears in order to succeed.

Tradition? – or The Inability to Grow

We have to learn to go new ways in order to continue with tradition. There is only one tradition that never changes. That is: "Everything changes over time!" In addition, we have to be able to adapt to change. There is a reason why the dinosaurs are not around anymore. They were much stronger than other animals. Other animals survived because they were able to adapt to the changes. Dinosaurs were not able to adapt and therefore did not survive. It shows that strength alone is a sure way to be extinct and wiped out. Survivors have been able to change with situations and circumstances. Real strength and power starts in your mind, not your arms.

"Like the dinosaurs, strength alone is a sure way to be extinct!"

How does this translate to a fight? You do not know what the attack will be. You also do not know how much power and the target of the attack. You pretty do not know anything besides the fact you are being attacked. Since you do not know anything about the actual attack, why would you want to choose a predetermined defense (such as a block) and hope it will work? This makes no sense. In addition, the attack can change in a split second without a warning. It is clear that you need to be able to adapt to an attack and be able to change your strategy and body position in a split second. As demonstrated and proven time and time again, the most effective method is the REVAT REFLEX TRAINING. This unique trainings method enables you to adapt to any attack in a split second and use the attacker's power to protect yourself. Talk to a certified Revat instructor to see and test this in person. This is the best way to really understand the powerful advantages and benefits of Revat. If you have martial arts training already, you can add the Reflex Training to your curriculum and it will make you much faster.

On a different note, how would you like your friends and family to see and remember you? It is up to you to create the personality you desire through your every day decisions and actions. Tough decisions in tough situations build character. Revat training can help you build that character. You can learn how to act and react under pressure and maintain control. Your life is all about the decisions you make. You are unique and only you can establish your position in society by being yourself. Revat training can help you to find your unique and successful personality.

"Tough decisions build character!"

Sometimes people hide behind the word 'tradition' because they are afraid of changes. Changes are good. We take advantage of changes every day. We drive better and safer cars, use the latest cell phone technology, computer and internet. Why should it be different when it comes to our personal safety and the safety of our family and loved ones?

"Safety is not isolation. It comes from within you."

Ingo Weigel

Everybody wants to live an eventful and exciting life with a lot of fun. However, many people are scared of the 'unknown'. Some people do not even know their neighbors.

Revat can be a huge part of our social life and our ability to interact with others. In fact, it allows us to have a social life. We love to go out to theaters, bars, nightclubs, concerts, private parties etc. Most of these events are usually in the evening and last throughout the night. Now, how many of you make plans on how to get home without becoming a victim of a robbery, rape or an assault of some sort? You walk with a friend, or better with two friends. However, what happens to the friend who is the last in this group? Let us just hope nothing happens to her or him. You try to get a taxi and hope that nothing happens to you when you get out of it and walk to your building. How about a concert or any other crowded place? Many things can happen while you are at the washroom and your friends are not with you because they do not want to miss the show.

You may think that the Police are there to help and protect you. Well, that is not really the whole truth. The Police and Law Enforcement are there to ensure public safety, not necessarily the individual person. Of course, they will protect you if they happen to be near you when you are attacked, but you cannot expect them to be there just for you. The people who protect individuals are called bodyguards. Good for you if you can afford a bodyguard. And if you can't afford one, you need to know Revat in order to help yourself and be safe.

With Revat, you acquire skills that will allow you to live your life the way you want to live it! Revat allows you to go out and have a social life. You can walk home at night without the fear of an attack. Through the unique design of the classes, you strengthen your confidence and your mental attitude to face new challenges in your professional and personal life.

We have developed a unique teaching curriculum to ensure that every student learns the complete program.

There is a need for new ways of learning self-defense and an even greater need for new and effective material and programs, such as Revat.

Revat – Recreation or Education?

We go to school to acquire basic knowledge in Mathematics, English, Foreign Languages, History, Biology, Physics, etc. After graduating, we move on and go to college to focus our education in a direction of our personal interest.

The Revat Technician Program is structured after the same model. In the beginner levels, students learn basic movements, techniques and their applications in self-defense situations. It does not make sense to teach self-defense at the end or as a special class because this is the number one reason why people start learning martial arts.

"Revat Self-Defense is a skill that can be learned like any other!"

The intermediate levels are considered "High School". Here a student expands his or her basic knowledge about self-defense, close combat fighting and starts with the reflex training. The Revat Reflex Training is one of the most effective ways to overcome a stronger and taller opponent by using his force against him.

The advanced levels are equivalent "College". Here the student deepens his education and, at the same time broadens his horizon with more sophisticated applications and scenarios. The knowledge and understanding of Revat is very important because things will start "coming together." Previous movements and applications become clearer; students get a much deeper understanding of the program and how to use their body to create more power. Furthermore, students will learn how to defend multiple opponents and attacks that involve weapons.

Revat is not only a recreational activity. On a deeper level, it is a sophisticated and educational program. In addition to explosive and effective self-defense, it also teaches about balance, relaxation, focus, discipline, persistence, patience and stress relief. It shows you how to solve problems. Like anything else in life, there is a time to learn and study and there is a time to apply the knowledge and have fun. Since life goes on, so must one's education.

Some people may think that education stops after graduation. I think it is almost the opposite. School education teaches a foundation of many subjects in order to get a start in life. It allows us to choose who we want to be in life. Real learning starts after graduation. We use the basic knowledge we have acquired in order to learn more and grow. We start life with a mass of theoretical knowledge and then it is time to see how much of this knowledge we actually understand by applying it practically.

"Revat is self-defense training and education on the physical, the mental and the spiritual level!"

We can analyze and research every topic in detail and still do not know how to do it. Success is the combination of theoretical knowledge and practical application. In other words, no matter how much theoretical knowledge we have accumulated over the years, it is only helpful if we can use that knowledge in practical situations to solve problems.

Why do we learn? We learn because we have goals in life. Any goal starts with a dream. We need to find a way to turn our dreams into reality. We start by gaining enough knowledge about a goal to get started. Mistakes cannot be avoided. It is important to make mistakes so we can learn from them and make better choices in the future. When you hit a wall, you know it is time to further deepen your theoretical knowledge in order to overcome that hurdle. This is how you proceed until you accomplish your goal.

Revat classes and instructions offer a great mix between theory and reality so the student gets two hundred percent back for one hundred percent invested.

What Kind of Self-Defense Training is Right for You?

The self-defense that works for you!

"Revat Self-Defense training gives you the skills and techniques to overcome a stronger and seemingly more powerful opponent."

Good techniques leverage the attacker's superior muscle strength and give you a real chance to protect yourself. Therefore, the regular person (man and woman) needs to benefit from self-defense training. It should complement you as a person; who you are and what you stand for.

If you are 6'5" and 250lb of pure muscle, do you actually need formal self-defense training? What I mean is the chances are much lower (almost zero) that you will be the victim of an assault or an attack; unless, of course you started the confrontation. Even if you're being attacked, no matter what you do will most likely work as means to defend yourself because you are already stronger and taller than most people. You only get in serious trouble if your attacker is even stronger and maybe even taller than you are; or if the other person (who is smaller than you are) has skills and techniques that leverage your strength to his advantage.

Revat self-defense training offers techniques and skills that can be learned and successfully applied by anyone. Self-defense training should not rely on one's muscle strength or body height. The smaller and weaker person needs good and reliable self-defense training. A stronger and taller attacker attacks the weaker and smaller person. Therefore, the smaller and weaker person needs to be able to apply self-defense techniques and these techniques have to work for the smaller and weaker person. Always!

Remember: The phrase "smaller and weaker" does apply to everyone. It is not a judgment of your state of physical fitness. It is in comparison to a potential attacker.

Traditional self-defense programs are based on muscle strength and have a low success rate for the regular person. Participants are bombarded with different techniques for different situations. They are supposed to remember all of them. It is also assumed that all techniques work for everyone equally. If a specific technique does not work then the participant needs to work harder and maybe think about adding some weight training to become stronger.

The point of good self-defense is to compensate and leverage these "disadvantages" and turn them into advantages. Therefore, Revat is based on principles that can be applied by anyone using the Revat Reflex Training.

Jennifer C.:

"Revat is right for me because I was looking for something that would build confidence, teach me how to instinctively react to danger as well as be a complete health and fitness program. It builds endurance, core body strength and focuses your mind and energy in a positive way. Revat develops mind-body coordination and trains your reflexes in a way that give you the confidence and skill to defend yourself."

Revat - Street (Self)-Defense

Revat is probably the most effective self-defense program available for professional adults.

Imagine you see two cats fighting and you tell both of them "...no biting, no scratching, no kicking below the waist, no hitting in the face and when you punch with your paw you need to turn your paw and throw your body in it ...". Of course, they are wearing special paw protecting gloves. The fight is set for 3 rounds of 5 minutes each round. After the fight, both fighters (or cats) are going to have a drink ("Got Milk?") and talk about their lethal and superior techniques. That is how many of today's martial arts and self-defense classes are structured.

Many martial arts have been altered over the years and have so many rules and regulations today that they have become useless. Their practitioners sometimes even have to wear a specific uniform that is necessary for some techniques. It is also necessary to warm up the muscles before "fighting" to avoid injuries.

"The more rules and regulations a specific style governs the higher is its dysfunction in real life self-defense situations."

Ingo Weigel

One of my very good friends is a black belt. He and some friends went to the Oktoberfest in Munich and they got into a fight with some other guys. He told me, all he did was staying very close to the guy he was fighting. He tried to punch him in any way possible. He knew that as long as he punched, the other guy could not punch him back because he had to defend the punches. That is what saved my friend, not his fancy techniques. After the fight, his friends asked him why he did not use the techniques he had practiced for many years. His answer was that there was not a good opportunity.

What instructors don't tell you is that their "self-defense" works only for certain people. It usually works for people 6ft and taller and 230+lb of muscle. The question should be: *"Do those people really need formal self-defense training?"*

What about the "regular" person who really needs to know how to defend him or herself? Are you out of luck? I do not think so. You need to know effective self-defense more than anyone else. A good self-defense program should not be based on muscle power or height.

What makes a good self-defense program reliable and effective? The program and training needs to adapt to an individual's height and ability to move. In addition, you need to be able to adapt to the attack as it happens, not as you wish it would happen. That brings us back to the importance of the Revat Reflex Training. Imagine if you would know what kind of attack is coming, how much force is in the attack and how determined the attacker is. Furthermore, you know what you have to do to defend this attack without getting hurt. Wouldn't that be a great position to be in when the fight starts? Would you be worried about the outcome of the fight? Would you even be worried if the attacker is stronger and taller than you are? Of course, you would not be worried. It would be as simple and comfortable for you as riding a bicycle.

"No street fight is fair!"

When you learned how to drive a car, it was new, maybe awkward or even scary. After you passed your driving test, you got your license and the world has been much brighter ever since. Today it does not matter to you if you are driving a big truck or a small car, a sports car or a family van. It is the same to you and you are not worried anymore. All you needed was proper instructions and the right training. You also did not go to a supermarket to sign up for driving lessons. You went to a driving school because you knew what you wanted to learn.

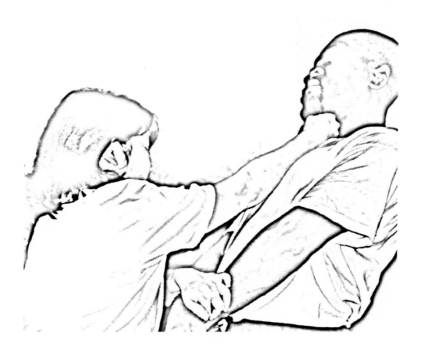

No street fight is fair! In a real fight, traditional martial art styles realize their weaknesses and try to compensate them with techniques from other styles such as boxing and wrestling, for example. It reduces some of these great martial arts to a collection of techniques without substance, interaction and much coordination. That is why they have '487' ways to defend a punch and '325' ways to defend a kick – and at the end they still get punched because they couldn't decide what technique to use. Not to mention that they can be punched or kicked from the right and/or from the left side. If someone has so many different options to choose from, he will be overwhelmed to make a decision in a split second.

In all fairness, I want to share with you that I have great respect and much interest in different kinds of martial arts. I am fascinated with their history, philosophy and traditions. It is exactly my deeper interest that leads me to great disappointment when I witness poor training and obviously very little understanding of the martial art itself. It is an open secret that over the years once great martial arts have been diluted and watered down by people who missed the point of the training. Their lack of interest, desire, effort and patience has lead to poor standards in today's martial arts schools as the number of "Weekend-Warrior" workshops and 6-months "Black belt" programs shows it. The desire for quick-fix solutions breeds a low level of quality that in the short term may seem feasible. However, as the past 30 years clearly show this low level of quality destroys great martial arts and reduces them to nothing but a color of a belt. Many adults and parents fail to see the benefits of high quality martial arts training. They could enjoy life on a level that is otherwise far out of reach, because it is something that you cannot but with money. However, this is a topic for another conversation. Let us return to reducing the reaction time to protect yourself.

"Unfortunately, once great martial arts have been reduced to nothing but a color of a belt!"

The time it takes to make this decision and to tell the body what to do is usually longer than the attacker needs for the actual punch or kick. The result is a painful awakening. It is not important how many techniques you know. It is, however important that you can actually use what you know in a real situation. Less is more!

This is a very important rule to remember. Revat is reflexive striking and reacting to an attack. Through the unique reflex training, these responses are implanted into the subconscious mind and muscle memory. You never know what kind of attack will come, how much power is behind this attack or if this is just a fake attack to distract and test you.

The only way to get reliable information about an attack is to get contact with the opponent's arms. Through the reflex training, you will be able to feel the pressure and react appropriately, instantly and proportionately; without it, you will always have to guess.

How Can You Benefit from Learning Revat?

There are many reasons why people learn Revat. The number one reason is the lack of their ability to defend themselves and their loved ones effectively. Other reasons are hobby, fun, meeting new people and personal growth. Some love working with people and become certified instructors.

It is difficult for beginners to find a good teacher. However, it also is as difficult to find a good student. Eagerness to deeper understanding, persistence and patience are not really striking characteristics in our society. As a result, not everyone is willing to practice regularly and explore Revat with all its benefits and advantages.

Revat has a lot to offer to people who have goals in life and are not afraid to pursue them. If you have to lead and manage people, if you have to make important decisions every day and if you prefer value over quick fix solutions, you will greatly benefit from learning Revat.

Revat itself can be learned quickly. The class environment encourages independent thinking and the use of your brain. Concentration, honesty and patience are necessary requirements for a better understanding of the program. Concentration means to focus on the presence. Honesty means to be critical with the skills learned and the ability to perform them. Patience is to train the movements until you can execute them reflexively in a stress situation.

It is well known that in times when the economy is down crime rates go up. People loose their jobs and do not know how to pay the bills and feed their families. They may feel they lost control and cannot see a way out.

Some become angry, even violent. You may hear about statistics that show that crime has gone down. However, this is not always the truth. The number of reported crimes may have gone down but this is because fewer crimes are reported. Local Law Enforcement is overwhelmed and does not have the work force to follow up on every report and every crime. They have no choice but to prioritize and do the best they possibly can. For example, if someone steals your purse or wallet would you really file a report? Moreover, even if you do, what are the chances the thug will be caught? Many people decide not to file a report. Hence, crime rates go down and a statistic shows that. Believe it at your own risk.

The best way to find out about Revat is to talk to a certified Revat instructor and attend an introduction class. This is a class designed for beginners to get hands-on information about Revat, its benefits and advantages, the instructors and the local school.

Revat in Real Life

Jennifer C.:

"Attitude: *Being confident is not being cocky. Knowing how to defend yourself does not mean go out and start a fight. Having the right attitude means being able to focus your energy, develop your mind and body coordination and hone your skills that will help you to defeat your opponent.*

Technique and Skills: *Balance, coordination, endurance, core strength come from training. Understanding the Form and movements and then learning how to apply them correctly and fluidly is critical and takes years to master."*

I have people asking me about Revat almost every day. When I tell them how Revat works, they seem disappointed and tell me that they "already" learned that in other martial arts classes. They also punch and kick, with fists and elbows and they step and move. And I start smiling...

Of course, it seems to be the same because the theory is same! Every human being has two arms and two legs. Now how many different ways of punching and kicking are there? Don't you think that by now all possible ways of punches and kicks have been discovered? So, what is the difference?

"Most self-defense instructions are in theory. Revat trains in reality! Revat is self-defense that works under psychological pressure in extreme situations!"

What does that mean? Simple, in theory everything works and everything is possible. Unfortunately, that is how many conventional martial arts and self-defense techniques are taught. Participants memorize certain patterns of movements. These patterns are supposed to represent a fight or an attack. With a little choreography, they can make it look very beautiful and impressive, just like in a Hollywood movie. However, at the end, it still is theory. The rude awakening comes when someone who does not use these patterns actually attacks them.

Revat trains under realistic circumstances because any attack is possible and therefore allowed. Anything can happen and there are no excuses. Revat trains the subconscious mind. Only that will allow you to truly react to any attack without having to make a conscious decision.

Beginners want to learn effective self-defense and certified Revat instructors are there to educate and teach them. A friendly and relaxed class environment is the basis for a successful and long lasting education.

From beginners, I hear quite often, that they were told to always run away if they get in a dangerous situation. As mentioned earlier, I am not sure this is always possible. It is not that simple because it is not realistic. Otherwise, we would not have any crimes, any rapes, no robberies, muggings, and no assaults. The attacked person could have just walk away. In fact, that statement would suggest the idea that a woman wanted to get raped because she chose not to walk away. As you can see it is just outrageous to say "...just walk away..."

So let us get back to reality. If a child is told to walk away from a confrontation, it starts thinking that this is the only way to solve the problem. "If there is a problem, I can just walk away!" When this child becomes an adult and is confronted with a difficult and challenging problem in the job, it remembers to walk away instead of confronting the problem and finding a solution.

"There is a time for diplomacy and a time for action."

If diplomacy does not show any results there is only action left. The key is to be in control. The only way to be in control is leadership. Leadership consists of confidence and the skills to take control. You always have a choice. Making the right choice depends on you! Let me explain this using the following two examples:

Let us say you walk down the street at night and a strange person walks towards you and demands your wallet. Most people are scared and freeze in these situations.

In order to make a good decision, you need to stay calm and in control. Just because the attacker is bigger, stronger or maybe has a weapon does not mean that he is actually in control. He thinks he is in control because you don't take charge.

Furthermore, let us assume you have formal training in Revat. You are calm and control the situation. You realize that you cannot walk away or avoid the situation. You have to deal with it. Being in control allows you to analyze quickly your options. Either you take on the attacker and eliminate him quickly using your Revat skills or you just give him your wallet and thank him for not hurting you physically. It is your decision.

Another example is in your job. Here we assume your boss approaches you and puts you in charge of a new project or getting a new client to work with you. You need to come up with a presentation for this client. However, you have never done anything like that before. Just like in the previous example, you can tuck your tail between your legs and tell your boss that you cannot do it because it is too difficult for you. In that case, your boss probably apologizes and asks you to stop by the HR department on your way out.

The other option is take on the challenge, grow with the project and find a solution for the problem. Whenever you doubt your abilities, keep in mind that your boss sees something in you that makes him believe that you can do it. If he did not believe in you, he would have given the project to someone else. This will calm you down and help you succeed.

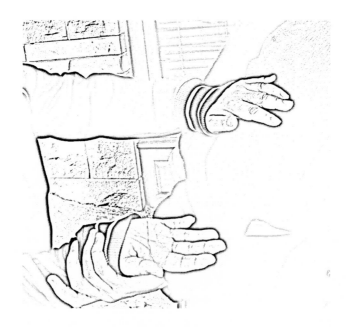

Revat teaches you to deal with all kinds of attacks from all kinds of attackers in all kinds of situations. Through this personalized and customized training, you gain the confidence to take on new challenges and grow with them. You gain the feeling of being unstoppable and you take this confidence with you. This will make you believe in yourself again and help you accomplish what you need to do.

.ne Brain and the Revat Reflex Training

The human brain is the center of the human nervous system and is the most complex organ. In oversimplified terms, we have three basic parts to our brain.

The left brain is generally used for reading, writing, speaking and logic. The right brain is often associated with pictures, music, art, creativity and imagination.

The subconscious brain is the most powerful brain because it includes the primitive brain. The primitive brain is most like an animal's brain. It does not think, but rather reacts, fights, flees, or freezes. The subconscious brain determines how we react in pressure situations. The subconscious brain affects our physical actions and reactions.

Techniques are stored in the left side of the brain. In traditional martial arts, practitioners train their techniques repetitively over many years of daily practice. However, only repetitive training is not enough to turn techniques into reflexes and move them from the left side of the brain to the subconscious brain. It requires to 'let go' of the predetermined techniques and allow your body to 'just react'; let things happen without consciously interfering. Only very few Masters of martial arts experience the shift from the left brain to the subconscious brain. For the majority of practitioners, this concept will always be foreign and even in theory hard to grasp and understand. It requires an above average willingness to learn and understand, a certain open-mindedness to new ideas and prioritize your training and education.

In today's world of instant gratification, these are very rare traits. Therefore, teaching curriculums have to be updated and modernized in order to be applicable under modern circumstances. At the same time, being a student of something still requires time, effort, willingness to learn and daily practice of the new material learned. Modern teaching programs do not eliminate the student's learning experience that comes from trial and error and the time invested to advance. This does not only apply to martial arts and self-defense. It also applies to college programs such as Business, Finances, professional sports and anything else.

In the beginning stages of learning Revat, the Reflex Training offers a structure for the beginner to practice the movements learned in the previous levels. In order to advance to a higher level, a practitioner needs to shift the focus of the training away from "doing" to "being". What does that mean? It means taking the techniques and movements from the left brain, getting creative with them (right brain) and ultimately moving everything to the subconscious brain. All of that is accomplished in the Revat Reflex Training.

Therefore, the Revat Reflex Training is essential to your ability to react in a split second effectively, appropriately, and efficiently when you find yourself in any stress situation.

The Science behind Revat

In order to apply proper science to Revat, we have to determine why it is important. Let us start with the center point.

In a fight, we have to protect the upper body and the head. All vital organs are somewhere in the body and head. It is not important where exactly they are located. The arms are placed on the left and the right side of the body in order to protect it from side impacts. You can find your center point by dividing your upper body in two equal halves vertically and horizontally. The center point is where these two lines cross.

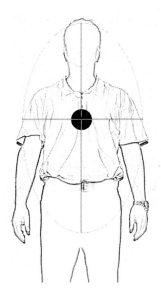

Your center point and the opponent's center point create the beginning and the end of the centerline in Revat. The centerline is the straight line between you and your opponent and represents the shortest distance.

When you extend your arms straight forward in front of your body and touch your hands your arms create a triangle. This triangle serves as a wedge, which is explained a little later in this chapter. Now you put your hands in the position as shown in the picture below.

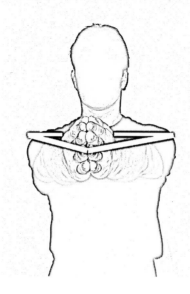

Now bend both of your elbows and move your hands in the position shown in the next picture. In that position, your arms create another triangle. The two triangles create a 3-dimensional protection shield in front of your body.

Now you have created the best protection you can get with your arms. Of course, the entire structure is of little use if you stand still and do not move. As soon as you start moving forward, your arms move with you and you are bound to make contact with your attacker.

A more scientific approach to self-defense makes the difference between being in control and being a victim. Scientific knowledge and applications leverage muscle strength and height differences. Throughout history, people always have searched for ways to be more effective. They applied scientific principles together with common sense to make hunting easier, to build bigger and safer homes, to protect themselves from enemies and nature and much more. Progress means moving forward.

The Revat Stance

Revat utilizes two stances, the pre-fighting stance and the close range stance.

The Pre-Fighting Stance: With your feet, you create a triangle. Your knees are being pushed together and your body weight is distributed equally on your feet. You sit on your legs, your hips are parallel to the floor and your body is straight upright. The fists are drawn back next to your chest and do not touch the body.

In this stance, you will find a natural balance of your body. It also can be a meditative stance and is used in the form training. The goal is to stand upright and relax the muscles. The lower back muscles need to be relaxed to avoid lower back pain. This is especially important for people who sit mostly in a chair and do not get much time to get up and stretch the body.

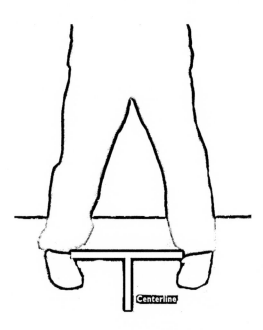

Centerline

If the stance is done right, it can help you correct your body's posture and prevent lower back pain.

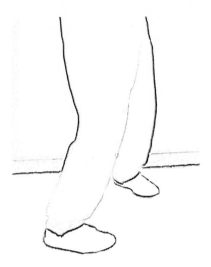

The body's weight is equally distributed between both feet. The entire foot has contact with the ground and the toes are relaxed.

Although this stance may feel awkward in the beginning, you will soon realize that this is a very comfortable stance. It gives your body a strong, yet flexible structure that is important to deflect much stronger forces.

The Close Range Stance: Your feet are placed in one line (centerline) towards your opponent. Knees are still pushed together and all the body weight is on your rear leg. There is no weight on the front leg. This allows you to defend low kicks immediately without having to shift your body's weight and loose time. This stance also helps you to maintain your balance and avoid being thrown to the ground Since the front foot is on centerline already, the defense will always be faster. The front leg protects the body below the waist and creates space between you and your attacker. Because of the body's weight distribution (zero weight on the front leg) a Revat practitioner will never loose balance when an opponent attempts to sweep his / her front or rear leg.

Some traditional martial arts instructors prefer a weight distribution of 90/10, 80/20 or even 70/30. Of course, this is nonsense for a couple of reasons. First, it is quite difficult to determine when 20% (or 10 or 30) of your body's weight are on your front leg.

Secondly, the footwork in Revat is very natural. When you walk down the street, you are shifting your body weight from one leg completely to the other leg (one hundred percent). Go ahead and try it. When you do not have to think about it, you will do it automatically. It is naturally the fastest way to move the body and change positions. Therefore, there is no other way than to distribute the body weight 100/0 in order to move quickly and naturally.

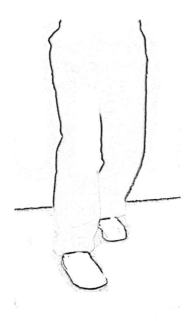

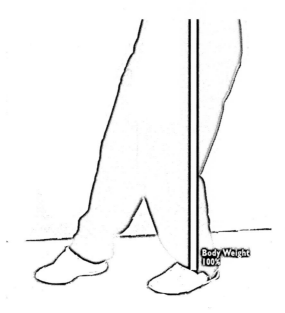

Body Weight 100%

The correct stance makes it virtually impossible to be surprised with a low kick. In this stance, a Revat practitioner reaches maximum stability and strengthens the leg muscles.

The Revat Footwork

The footwork is very important and essential in a fight. Top athletes improve their skills by improving their footwork.

When we learned how to walk, it was awkward in the beginning and we fell down quite often. However, the more we tried the better we became and the easier it was for us to stay on both feet.

Then we have learned climbing stairs and running. Once we were able to run, we began participating in different kinds of sports such as football, basketball, soccer, Baseball, Track and Field and many more.

The more we used our feet to move around the more natural it felt. The awkwardness from the early beginnings was long gone.

In Revat, we approach the footwork the same way. In the beginning, it may feel awkward and different. Nevertheless, the more a student uses the footwork the easier it gets and the more natural it feels. There are no low and difficult stances, as they exist in conventional martial arts that make it very difficult to move. In conventional martial arts, the focus is on a strong stance that can withstand incoming forces and attacks. This is beautiful if you are stronger than your opponent is. However, what if you are not? Then you are run over by the attacker and you will be overwhelmed because you are not prepared and cannot move fast enough. Some of you may think the solution is lifting weights to become stronger. That is only a short-term solution because you are playing the game by someone else's rules. You are chasing the idea of being the strongest person. Why not force the opponent to play your game? Show him that muscles are not the answer to explosive self-defense. It all starts with the footwork.

The Power of the Revat Punch

The Revat punch is extremely fast and powerful. It shoots forward on a straight line and offers maximum power and protection due to its elbow position. The Revat punch utilizes a vertical fist instead of a horizontal fist position. Elbow and shoulder stay strong and do not collapse at the time of impact. The practitioner can put his entire body behind the punch without loosing flexibility and balance.

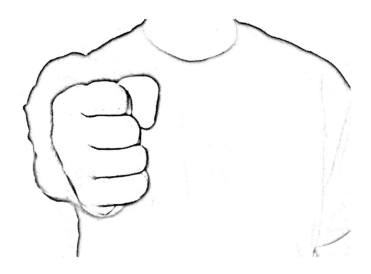

Let me explain this on the following example. Go in a deep and strong stance (like a Karate stance for example) and extend your arm like a punch straight forward. Turn your fist horizontal and ask someone to push against your fist. You will realize that this kind of punch is only as strong as your shoulder and upper arm muscles.

Now, you can pick the same stance or the close range stance from Revat. Put your arm straightforward, turn your fist vertical and you even can bend your elbow. Let your elbow hang downwards in a natural position. Again, have someone push against your arm. Here you will see that it is much easier for you to withstand the incoming force. In other words, the person who pushes has to use much more strength just to move your arm a little.

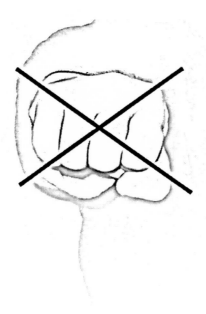

If the fist is horizontal (like in many traditional martial arts), the punch is only as strong as the arm and the shoulder. The first joint that usually collapses in that kind of punch is the elbow. Therefore, people start lifting weights to increase the muscles. Through that, the punch usually becomes slower unless they train the speed of the punch. This is an option if you have several hours each day for your training. Moreover, with increasing age it becomes harder and harder to maintain this routine. Of course, if you put in the effort it takes and train hard you will develop a very powerful punch.

Boxers are the perfect example. Although they use a horizontal fist position for their punches, they are extremely fast and powerful. Most people do not have the time to train as boxers do. They need to leverage their time more efficiently. As an interesting side note, when professional boxers still fought without gloves they also used the vertical fist position. It changed once boxing rules required wearing boxing gloves in the ring.

The unique chain punches in Revat are one of the most effective and powerful weapons. You will learn these punches in the very beginning so even as a beginner you can use them when necessary. It is very difficult to block or otherwise defend these punches with common methods. Revat chain punches are an endless series of punches. While punching, the student keeps maximum protection to be ready for possible counterattacks. A trained practitioner of Revat is able to throw 4 – 6 punches (or even more) per second. Everybody can learn to do that regardless of age or sex.

The Revat Sparring

The sparring in Revat is very important and somewhat different from regular sparring. It offers the opportunity to train all the movements and techniques learned so far in a realistic, yet controlled environment. There are two different ways to spar in Revat:

Reflex Sparring to Learn: This is the kind of sparring practiced in the beginner levels. It means that a beginner learns to apply all the techniques he or she has learned so far without the fear of getting hurt. A qualified instructor can help a beginner to correct mistakes. The speed is slow enough for the beginner to see the movements and react accordingly. It also increases the beginner's confidence in the techniques learned. Punches to the head and face are avoided.

"He who has control has Power!"

Reflex Sparring to Fight: This sparring is much faster and requires a higher level of control. At this level, it is impossible for the practitioners to see the movements. Movements and techniques are felt through the tactile reflexes trained in the Revat Reflex Training. This kind of sparring offers a great full body workout and improves your cardio. You will learn to move and react at a very high speed in the close range distance. You are in constant contact with your sparring partner. Anything is possible: punches, elbows, kicks whatever you can think of. Of course, all movements and techniques are still controlled. Nobody is supposed to get a black eye or a broken nose. Control is everything! Sparring is not a brawl. It is a way of learning and increasing skills.

A fight can happen in <u>five different distances</u>:

1. The Kicking distance (longest range)

2. The Punching distance

3. The Knee and Elbow distance

4. The Wrestling distance (no actual wrestling! But rather how to defend wrestling attacks and take downs)

5. The Anti-Ground Fight

Conventional martial arts usually focus on the fight in one or two distances. They are vulnerable if they have to fight someone who is more familiar with a different distance. Mixed Martial Arts are not much different. When the fighters stand on their feet, they punch and kick and when they are on the ground, they wrestle. They mix two or more conventional martial arts and the result is still conventional martial arts fighting, naturally.

In Revat, you will learn to fight and defend attacks in any and all five distances while using the same techniques and movements. The Revat principles apply in all five distances. Revat teaches you to defend all kinds of attacks in any of the five distances. This is the focus of the program starting in the beginner levels. From the first day beginners learn realistic close quarter combat fighting and self-defense that is reliable, explosive and highly effective.

"Never box with a boxer! And never wrestle with a wrestler!"

The Revat Reflex Training gives you the ability to control a situation, a fight and of course, the opponent. If you know how to maintain control, you can also control the attacker's movements and his ability to attack again, but more importantly and because of your training, you determine the outcome of this confrontation.

Revat puts you in control of the situation and the fight!

In a fight, you naturally go through the distances systematically. That means you will be able to use them all if necessary. Usually the fight ends in the knee and elbow range (the third distance). A real fight cannot take long, only a few seconds. The longer a fight takes the higher the chances that you get hit too.

The Revat Reflex Training

The Revat Reflex Training is the missing link to effective and reliable close quarter combat fighting. With this specific trainings program practitioners train their reflexive responses to different attacks and movements initiated by the attacker. Revat practitioners are able to react according to touch, pressure and force that stems from an attack. Reflexive responses eliminate the decision making process that is required and necessary in conventional programs. Therefore, it does not matter what kind of attack is threatening you or how much force is in this attack. With Revat, you would not resist to the incoming force from an attack. Instead, you would allow the attacker to move your body (his target) out of the way by using his own force. It sounds simple and it is just that. Anybody can learn it and apply it successfully.

You will get physical contact because the attacker is trying to hurt you. Once, the contact is made you will know how much force is in that attack and the direction of it. You can use this information to control the attacker and move your body so you do not get hurt. That is what the Revat Reflex Training is all about; it gives you control over the opponent and the situation. It puts you in charge. If you do not get physical contact... well then there is no physical self-defense needed!

Here is another interesting fact. Since Revat self-defense is based on touch and tactile reflexes, the reflexive self-defense response to an attack is always performed with appropriate force.

The reflex training is the heart of Revat. This kind of training is unique and highly effective on many levels. Here you will learn to feel the pressure and force of the opponent's attack and to react appropriately and proportionately. The Revat Reflex Exercises are not a fight! They are used to train the reflex system, to improve the ability to feel pressure and react to it, to coordinate your arms and legs and to get a great workout. Revat practitioners train all attacks and reflexive defenses in a very close range. They learn to move according to the opponent's attacks and pressure. The proper reflex training gives you the ability and skills to dominate any close range fighting situation.

The Revat Reflex Training is a very social learning process and fun for everyone. Reflexive techniques should be practiced as relaxed as possible without any muscle tension. A certain forward pressure is present at all times. Only in the right environment and under qualified supervision is it possible to gradually develop effective skills and go from 'doing fast' to 'being fast'. A student's personal growth will expand with the development of his or her reflexive skills.

It is easy to understand the theory of the Revat principles. Only through honest observation of yourself and ongoing training with a qualified instructor can the knowledge be converted into practical applications. Applying the explosive and highly effective Revat techniques in a real life situation does not require a warm-up or stretching. The reason is simple. There is no time on the street to warm-up and make the attacker wait until you are ready. You need to be able to defend an attack immediately; no matter where you are, who attacks you, whether your hands are occupied, you are sitting down, standing in an elevator or a crowded place, whether you are on the train or wherever you may be. The only way to protect yourself and your loved ones effectively is by using the natural movements taught in Revat. The proper training will turn techniques into reflexes.

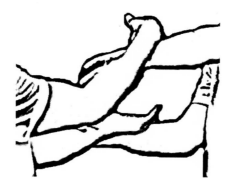

How Can You Get More Information?

In order to get more information please visit:

www.RevatInt.com

www.FreeSelfDefenseAdvice.com

You can watch video clips, find a Revat Training Center near you and get information on classes, corporate workshops and instructor certification levels. You also can hire a certified Revat instructor and mentor to work with you.